The
Self Publishing Field Guide

Dr. Roger D Smith

Modelbenders Press

The Self Publishing Field Guide

Copyright 2010 by Roger Smith. All rights reserved. No part of this book may be reproduced or transmitted in any form or by any means, electronic or mechanical, including photocopying, recording, or by any information storage and retrieval system, without written permission from the author. For information address Modelbenders Press, P.O. Box 781692, Orlando, Florida 32878.

Modelbenders Press books may be purchased for business and promotional use or for special sales. For information please contact the publisher.

PRINTED IN THE UNITED STATES OF AMERICA

Visit our web site at www.modelbenders.com

Designed by Adina Cucicov at Flamingo Designs

The Library of Congress has cataloged the paperback edition as follows:
Smith, Roger
   The Self Publishing Field Guide
   Roger Smith. – 1st ed.
   1. Authorship—Marketing 2. Authors and Publishing
   3. Publishers and Publishing
   I. Roger Smith II. Title

ISBN: 978-0-9843993-1-4

Also by Roger Smith

Advice: Written on the Back of a Business Card
Texts 2 Teens: Sending the Advice and Wisdom That They Desperately Need
Fortune Cookies: Small Secrets on How to Make a Fortune

Becoming the Millionaire Employee
The Millionaire Employee Investment Guide
Overcoming the 4 Failures: Stupid, Lazy, Ugly & Afraid
In the Footsteps of Franklin

Chief Technology Officer: Defining the Responsibilities of the Senior Technical Executive
Military Simulation and Serious Games: Where We Came From and Where We Are Going
Game Technology in Medical Education: An Inquiry into the Effectiveness of New Tools
Simulation Interoperability: Challenges in Linking Live, Virtual, and Constructive Systems

Trademark Usage

The following trademarks are referenced in the text of this book. Each mark is the property of its respective owner:

- 1-and-1
- Amazon.com
- Barnes & Noble Nook
- Barnes & Noble PubIt
- Bing
- Blogger
- Bowker
- Corel Office
- Dreamhost
- eBay
- Elance
- Facebook
- FedEx
- Go Daddy
- Google
- Google Docs
- Half.com
- iFreelance
- InDesign
- iStockphoto
- Kinko's
- Lightning Source
- Live Journal
- LogoTournament.com
- Lulu
- Microsoft
- Microsoft Office, Word, PowerPoint, and Excel
- Moo.com
- MySpace
- OpenOffice
- PayPal
- Project4Hire
- ThinkFree
- United States Postal Service
- VistaPrint
- Wikipedia
- Word Press
- Zoho Writer
- Yahoo!

TABLE OF CONTENTS

Foreword	3
Part I: Writing	5
Chapter 1: Your Story	7
Chapter 2: The Words	13
Chapter 3: Copyright Right	19
Chapter 4: Get the Picture	25
Part II: Publishing	35
Chapter 5: Hiring Help	37
Chapter 6: 100% Proof	55
Chapter 7: Great Designs	63
Chapter 8: Take a Number	69
Chapter 9: Finding Gutenberg	75
Chapter 10: Talley Ho!	89
Part III: Promoting	93
Chapter 11: You the Publisher	95
Chapter 12: Promoted	99
Chapter 13: Untangling the Web	107
Chapter 14: Logo Therapy	115
Chapter 15: Adding it Up	121
Chapter 16: FaceSpace	125
Chapter 17: The Big Show	131
Chapter 18: Aaaaa Bbbbb Aaaaa	137
Part IV: Selling	141
Chapter 19: Navigating the Amazon	143
Chapter 20: Money Money Money	147
Chapter 21: Wrap it Up	155
Part V: Legalizing	161
Chapter 22: To the Library	163
Chapter 23: Leaving Your Mark	171
Chapter 24: Home Away From Home	179
Chapter 25: Ink Inc	183
Chapter 26: End of the Beginning	191

FOREWORD

The primary topic of this book is turning your manuscript into a printed book. That is the focus of "Part II— Publishing". But my own experience in writing, publishing, and promoting books motivated me to include guidance on the supporting topics as well.

"Part I—Writing" provides a few tips on finding the tools and resources that can help you to write and illustrate your manuscript. If you already have a finished manuscript in your hand, then feel free to leap straight to the Publishing section.

"Part II—Publishing" is the real meat of this book. It describes where and how to hire the help that you need to turn your manuscript into an electronic file that complies with the requirements of a book printer. It describes the advantages of hiring a proof reader to insure that your work is readable by the rest of the English speaking world. Then I guide you through getting an ISBN for your book and working with an on-demand printer. At the end of this section of the book, you will be ready to order your first copies from the printer.

"Part III—Promoting" covers the importance of marketing your book to build a readership. So many books are published every day that you cannot get noticed unless you are putting real effort into drawing attention to your work.

"Part IV—Selling" describes some of the options that you have for fulfilling orders. You can do it yourself, or allow other companies to do it for you. There are advantages to both methods. You need to understand your responsibilities in order to choose which is best for you.

"Part V—Legalizing" covers issues associated with copyright registration, trademarks, and incorporating your publishing business. These details are not especially important when you are getting started, but they will become necessary when you have been successful with your first book and want to continue to grow your little empire.

You will start reading this book as an author, but will finish as an author, publisher, promoter, and small business person.

Feel the rush.

PART I

Writing

A few words on finishing your manuscript.

Chapter 1

Your Story

Part I: Writing

Benjamin Franklin was a serial self-publisher of *Poor Richard's Almanac*. Thomas Payne inflamed the American Revolution by self-publishing *Common Sense*. Walt Whitman changed modern poetry when he self-published *Leaves of Grass*. Richard Bolles taught the world to get a job when he self-published *What Color is Your Parachute?* Jack Canfield launched a huge series of bestsellers when he self-published *Chicken Soup for the Soul*.

All of these people had a burning desire to share their message with the world—just like you do. Each of them launched their manuscripts into print by deciding to take the publishing job on themselves. Now it is your turn to do the same.

Most people do not know how to begin the publishing process. This "cookbook for books" will walk you through every step of the process. You will create your own finished book in just two months.

This is not about how you might be lucky enough to get your manuscript accepted by a large and generous publisher. It is an instruction manual for making it happen yourself. You will become your own small publishing company. You will promote your work to readers. You will attract the attention of the larger publishers.

Start today and have your own book in just two months.

Two Lives

We all live two lives. First, there is the life where events happen to us every day. This is what most people call the "real world". Then there are the stories that play in our mind while we are living in that "real world." While the real world is largely beyond our control, our mental world is uniquely under our control. We can control everything about this second world and it is just as valuable to us as the first world that everyone is talking about.

For literalists, their second life is in lock step with their first life. What happens in their minds is synchronized with the real world. Then there are the romantics who base their second life on the real world, but make it much more colorful, hopeful, and exciting. Finally, at the extreme edge of this group are the fantasists whose second life has only the thinnest connection to what is happening in the real world. The story these people are living in their minds is a fascinating and enthralling escape from the real world.

You are reading this book because you want to tell your second life to the real world. If you are a literalist you might have a fact-based, how-to book in mind. If you are a romantic you might want to write a fictionalized version of your own life. If you are a fantasist you want to paint a picture of an entirely new universe.

But all of you have a story that you want to tell.

Maybe your story is already written down. Maybe it has been for months or years. But there is a brick wall between your manuscript and a published book that you can release to the world. You and thousands of writers just like you are looking for a door in that brick wall. You need someone to help you find, open, and walk through the door that leads to a published book. In this book I will show you that door, unlock it, and escort you down the hall to where your own printed book is waiting. If you follow me down this hall you will be holding your first case of books in just two months. Shall we take the journey together? Are you ready to turn the dream of your published book into a reality? Are you ready to introduce your second life to the real world?

Publishing World

All aspiring authors are intimidated by the publication process. The big companies looking down on you from the skyscrapers of New York City seem unapproachable and uninterested. Thousands of authors have approached the fortress of book publishing and been turned away. They all carry the pain of repeated rejection letters burned into their hearts. They have given up and returned to their day jobs while their story is dying within them.

But this is the 21st century and the book publishing process has been liberated. You do not have to wait for someone else to give you permission to publish your book. In the 21st century, you can do the entire process yourself. The printed book that emerges will be just as beautiful and exciting as anything that a New York publisher would create. You just need a guide to show you the path. You do not need my permission. You do not need permission from New York City. You just need your own permission to make this happen.

If you can write a book—you can publish a book.

If you have the energy, discipline, and intelligence to write—you have the energy, discipline, and intelligence to publish.

The Book Cookbook

The Self Publishing Field Guide does not present a dozen different ways that you might try to hopefully reach publication someday. *The Self Publishing Field Guide* is a cookbook about how to do it yourself in just a couple of months. If you can follow the recipe for a birthday cake, you can follow the recipe to get your book published.

I will tell you exactly what you need to do. I will point you to the essential services that will help you. I will give you a realistic budget and schedule to reach the end.

Once you read this book, the only thing that can stop you from publishing your book are your own excuses.

Part I: Writing

The Self Publishing Field Guide will show you everything that you need to know to move from a draft manuscript to a case of printed books in your hands in just a couple of months.

The Self Publishing Field Guide will transform you from an aspiring author to a published author.

I have used this process to publish all of my own books. It has worked for me and it can work for you.

With an investment of two months and about $1,000 you can have your own book.

It is time to put your second life into print and release it into the real world.

> *"Whatever your mind can conceive and believe it can achieve."*
> **—Napolean Hill, 1960**

At the end of each chapter you will find a text box that summarizes the time and money needed to accomplish the steps in that chapter. You can use this to watch your book come into existence one step at a time.

Money	Time
About $12 to purchase this book.	A few hours to read it.

Chapter 2

The Words

Before we jump into the publication process, I want to give you a little help with the writing process. If you have already finished your manuscript then you can skip to Part II. But if you still have all or part of your writing to do, then you might learn something new here.

Tools of the Trade

In the 21st century you do not need a typewriter or a stack of notebooks to write a book. Instead you need a computer and a word processing program. You do not need reference books, you need reference web sites. You do not need postage and envelopes, you need an internet connection.

If you have a computer and an internet connection, then you are all set. If you cannot afford these, then there are a number of places where you can get them for free. The most common place is the public library. The second is your place of employment. Finally, you can ask your community to give you one. Post an advertisement on Craig's List or Freecycle. Explain that you are an author who cannot afford to purchase a computer and ask for someone to donate their used machine to you for free. You will get it.

Word Processing

There are several great word processing programs that most authors use to write their book. These are fantastic tools for writing, formatting, and correcting your work. The most popular is obviously Microsoft® Word® which is part of the Microsoft® Office® suite of tools. This has become the universal standard for creating and editing written electronic documents.

As an aspiring writer you qualify to purchase Microsoft® Office® suite for only $150. This is not free, but it is a great bargain over the retail price to businesses.

However, Office® has been so successful that there are a number of imitators. There are commercial products like Corel® Office® and there are free alternatives. Some of these mimic Office® in every single feature. Others attempt to create only the most popular and powerful features. All of them allow you to save documents in a format that is compatible with Microsoft® Office®.

You may be surprised to learn that a number of these programs are completely free.

OpenOffice

My favorite alternative is OpenOffice. It is a freeware program that was developed to mimic Office®. It contains almost every feature that you will find in Microsoft Word®, PowerPoint®, Excel®, and several other programs. Documents written with OpenOffice can be saved in Word® format, which makes it easy to exchange your documents with the editors that you will be hiring later in the process.

Aside from brand preference, there really is no reason for an author to pay $150 for the Microsoft® product when you can have almost exactly the same capability for free. Writers, students, business people, and average citizens around the world have discovered this and have downloaded over 100 million copies of this program.

OpenOffice is a big software package just like Microsoft® Office®, so give it plenty of time to download on your home computer network.

> Download OpenOffice at: http://www.openoffice.org/

Google Docs

If you do not want to download a big program and install it on your computer, you can use a web-based word processor. This program will run inside of a web browser and without any installation on your own computer. The most popular of these is Google® Docs®. This provides the most essential word processing capabilities, but does not copy everything that can be done with OpenOffice.

Google Docs will save your documents to your online Google account, or you can download them to your own computer. If you choose to store your documents online you can access them from any computer that is connected to the internet. All you have to do is log in to your Google account and open the document that is stored there. This will allow you to write from a computer at work, at home, in a hotel, or at a friend's house. In every case you are always connecting to the same document no matter where you log in from.

> **Access Google Docs at: http://docs.google.com/**

If you are going to use Google Docs you have to create a free Google account. This will also give you access to their email, photo storage, and a host of online programs.

Other Options
There are several more online document editing programs like Google Docs®. Many of these have been around longer than the Google product, but they just have not had the same level of advertising and exposure. Each of them has about the same features, advantages, and disadvantages. You might want to check them out if you have a problem using OpenOffice or Google Docs.

> **Zoho® Writer at: http://www.zoho.com/**
> **ThinkFree® at: http://member.thinkfree.com/member/go-AboutService.action**

Resources
There was a time when a writer needed a number of reference books to be able to look up essential information about the history of ancient Greece, the difference between fairies and nymphs, and the street layout of New York City.

That was the 20th century. In the 21st century we use the internet.

Part I: Writing

Today you can find almost all of the information that you need at one of the millions of internet web sites. Most research for writing can be carried out for free. You can start looking for any piece of information with a search engine like Google, Yahoo!, or Bing.

You can also dip into a rich encyclopedia at Wikipedia®. There are several great books of quotations online as well.

> **Wikipedia® Encyclopedia: http://en.wikipedia.org/**
> **Books of Quotes: Great-Quotes.com, BrainyQuote.com, or WisdomQuotes.com**

Everything that was ever written is not online... not yet. There is still a wealth of factual, business, and scientific data that is only available in print, or only on pay-for-service web sites. If you are writing a book on a specific topic that deals with this information, you probably already know about these resources and may even subscribe to them.

All you need is a computer, internet connection, word processor, and a few internet resource sites to get started writing a great book. The cost of all of these can be extremely low or completely free. There is no reason to let any of them hold you back from creating your book.

Money	Time
OpenOffice Word Processing Software—$0.	Download OpenOffice—1 day to download, install, and setup.

Chapter 3

Copyright Right

Part I: Writing

Do you know that you have instant ownership and copyright to anything that you write? Your books and chapters are just like handmade furniture. A woodworker combines wood, stain, tools, and his own labor to create a chair that is a unique product of his own hands. Your books are exactly the same. When you create them, they belong to you. However, if someone has hired you to write the material as part of a job, then this is a "work for hire." If they are paying you, then the book belongs to them just like a chair made in a factory belongs to the company, not to the employee. But when you create your own book, you can tag it as copyrighted by you.

Where do you put that copyright label?

Just inside of every book is a title page and on the back of that you will find the "Copyright Page." This contains details about the owner and publisher of the book. It also contains cataloging data to help bookstores and libraries place it in the correct section of the store or the web site.

The copyright page confuses many people because they are not sure what it means or what they should report there. You can make this page as simple or as complicated as you like. At a minimum it should contain the statement of who owns the copyright, the address of the publisher, cataloging information, and the ISBN.

Copyright Statement

The copyright statement should identify the author of the work and the year in which it was completed. This can be written in many forms, to include:

Copyright © 2010 by Roger Smith
© 2010, Roger Smith
Copyright 2010 by Roger Smith

You can look at the many variations of this in one of the books on your own shelves. Pick the form that you like the best and go with it. In the Legalizing section of this book I will discuss the protection that this simple copyright statement gives you. I will also discuss some reasons that you might want to register your copyright with a government agency.

Publishers Address

The address of the publisher tells people who want to order directly from the publisher where to send their inquiries. It also helps the news media contact you for interviews.

Traditionally the address has been a postal or street address. But increasingly, a web site URL is included because it is so much more useful. I recommend that you include both a postal mailing address and a web site address. As the author you may feel that you do not have either of these. You might be reluctant to share your home street address with the readers of the world and I believe you are right to be cautious about this.

Publishers usually have their own unique web sites and mailing addresses. If you are self-publishing the book then you should consider creating your own post office box and web site. I discuss this in more detail in the Promoting section of this book.

Contributions and Ownerships

Your book may contain pictures or trademarked terms that need to be acknowledged. Explicit statements on this appear on the copyright page. In my own books I usually identify the layout artist who has created the book and give attribution to any quote or picture that appears on the cover.

The Fair Use section of the Copyright laws of the United States allow you to quote short sections from other works without asking permission from the author or publisher. If you use longer pieces from previous works you will need to get permission and include a statement to that effect on the copyright page.

Cataloging Information

Your book is one of millions in print. When it arrives at a bookstore, library, or web site, they do not read the whole book to figure out where it should go in the catalog or on the shelves. Instead they turn to the "Subject Category" that you have included on the copyright page and in the publication records.

You do not create new and unique categories for your own work. It does not help Amazon.com to see that your book is categorized as "Left handed taffy pullers." This may describe the main topic of the book. But it is not one of the standard categories where it can be grouped other similar books. The subject categories you will use come from a list that is maintained specifically for book publishers, distributors, and retailers. These categories exist to help place the book in an area where it will encounter the most interested readers.

The book you hold in your hands was printed by Lightning Source Inc (LSI). I used their online cataloging tools to select the categories to be associated with this book. That list is licensed from the Book Industry Study Group's "BISAC Subject Heading" catalog. If you want to look through all of these subject categories you can browse them at:

http://www.bisg.org/what-we-do-0-136-bisac-subject-headings-list-major-subjects---2009-edition.php

When you are uploading your book files to Lightning Source's web site you will use several of their web-based forms to describe the book. One of these forms allows you to select three Subject Categories for your book. For this book I selected:

1. Authorship—Marketing
2. Authors and Publishing
3. Publishers and Publishing

You can play with the forms to find all of the subjects that already exist for the keywords that you have in mind. Selecting the subject categories is part of the printing process that is described later.

ISBN

The last essential piece of data to appear on the copyright page is the ISBN, or International Standard Book Number. Every book has its own unique number to identify it among the millions of competitors. Later we will walk through the process of purchasing one or more of these identification numbers. For your first draft you can just put "XXXX." Later your book designer will help you insert the appropriate number in all of the places that it should appear in your book.

Infinite Variety

The amount of information that can potentially appear on this page is constantly growing. This is where publishers communicate information that is beyond the content of the book. Some publishers like to tout the fact that the book is printed on recycled paper, others like to invite large organizations to order the book at a discount. None of this is essential or required.

You might create your first copyright page by imitating the contents of the copyright page in this book and adjusting it for your own work.

Money	Time
No costs for this step.	1 day to layout your copyright page.

Chapter 4

Get the Picture

A picture is worth a thousand words. That is why a picture is the perfect descriptor for the cover of a book. You can't fit the entire summary of the book on the cover, but a good picture can tell a big part of your story.

Many authors use pictures on the cover and in the chapters to convey their message more clearly. It is always a treat to find a picture at the beginning of each chapter or in the middle of a long piece of text. As a self-publisher you have access to thousands of professional photographs and illustrations to include in your book, but you probably just do not know it yet.

Where can you find all of these illustrations? How can you license them? Do you have to hire an artist to create a unique illustration for you? Read on to get the answers to these questions.

Stock Photos and Illustrations

When you include pictures in your printed book, you cannot simply snatch them from the millions of web pages on the internet. The legal restrictions on books are much stricter than using purloined pictures in business presentations and birthday cards. Most of the images that you find on the web belong to an artist or a company and cannot be used legally in printed materials without paying a licensing fee. However, it is almost impossible to locate the legal owners of those images to ask their permission and work out a deal. You need to find a marketplace where artists and photographers are actively licensing their works for use. You do not want to use Google

Image Search or any similar engine to find images, photos, and illustrations to place in your book. That could land you in legal trouble.

The best place to look for illustrations is on one of the many stock photo and illustration markets on the web. Each of these contains thousands of images that are available for licensing at very reasonable prices. With just a few minutes of searching you will find dozens of images to consider for your book.

> **Stock Photo web sites:**
> Istockphoto.com
> FotoSearch.com
> ShutterStock.com
> Illustrationworks.com
> Images.com

I am very familiar with the istockphoto.com web site. That is where I found the images that I used in my last twelve books. It is easy to use, includes several helpful tools, and the licensing fees are very reasonable.

Creating an account at iStockphoto® is free and opens the door to millions of images. These images are categorized as either photos or illustrations. Each one has been tagged by the contributor with keywords that describe the image. The site also links terms together that have similar meanings. Therefore, when you are searching, try to think like the artist of the photo or illustration. How would they tag the image that you are looking for? Do not search for the terms that describe what you are doing with the picture, but rather what an artist would use to describe their work.

If you have searched the internet for images, you have developed a feel for the kinds of terms that work best to find what you are looking for. That same feel will serve you well when searching iStockphoto.

For example, one of my previous books contained short words of advice that could be text messaged to teenagers' cell phones. I started by searching iStockphoto for terms like "teenage cell phone". This led to many images of cell phones and quite a few posed pictures of happy teenagers using their cell phones. The latter was exactly what I was asking for and applied directly to the idea of the book. But the pictures did not convey the right feeling for the book. I wanted to get across the idea that a parent is trying to break through the barriers that teenagers erect around taking advice. I needed something that pointed toward that remote, separated clique of teenagers. I found this by searching for illustrations tagged as "teenage groups" rather than photos, and made no mention of the term "cell phone." This led me to an illustration containing the shadowy outlines of a group of teenagers who appeared to be separate and difficult to identify. This was perfect for the idea behind the book. But it took dozens of searches spread out over several days for my mind to release the term "cell phone" and dig deeper into groups of teenagers.

Licensing Fees

When you find an image that you like, you can purchase the right to use that image in your work.

If the image will appear on the cover of the book then you need one of the larger sizes with a high resolution. This would be either the Large or Medium sized image as listed on the site. The prices of each image vary based on how difficult it was for the artist to create the image, how rare and unique it is, and the level of resolution.

For example, I found a photo of a stack of books entitled "Big Pile of Books". The large version of this photo is 2592 x 3872 pixels, or 8.6" x 12.9" at 300 dpi resolution. Printed books require a resolution of 300 dots per inch to be crystal clear when they appear on paper. The large version of this image can be licensed for 15 credits.

Licensing fees at iStockphoto are expressed in credits instead of dollars for a couple of reasons. First, you purchase credits from the site and use these to purchase the images themselves. If you are going to buy a lot of images, then you buy a big block of credits and receive a discounted price for them. This means that heavy users receive a better deal than someone who is just there to get a single image. Second, these images are licensed all over the world. There are versions of this web site in many foreign countries, languages, and currencies. The credit system creates an exchange rate that allows the images to be sold in many different currencies. "Big Pile of Books" costs 15 credits in every country. But the translation of these credits into dollars, pounds, euros, kronars, bat, won, and yen is only done once, rather than millions of times through the entire catalog.

One reason that I use iStockphoto is that my book layout artist lives in a different country. I need a site that she can access and from which she can purchase images in her own currency. So I select an image from the site, send her the reference number, and she purchases the right sized image using her own account on iStockphoto.

Let's assume that I am going to use the "Big Pile of Books" image on the cover of my next book. That is going to cost 15 credits. But I might also include ten smaller images on the inside as illustrations at the beginning of each chapter. I might be able to license each of these in the Small or Medium size for just 5 or 10 credits. That means that my entire bill for images is 115 credits.

If you visit the "Buy Credits" page of istockphoto you will find that a package of 120 credits is available for $170, or about $1.42 per credit. So it might cost you $170 for the images you need.

Or it might not cost you anything. Keep reading before you buy.

Book Layout Fees

In a later chapter we describe the process of hiring a book layout designer. This is the person who will turn your manuscript into an electronic file that looks the same as the printed book. An expense that is generally covered by the layout fees is the licensing of a reasonable number of images, one of which is the cover image. My own layout artist typically figures in the cost of about ten images when pricing a project. If I ask for more images or I select something that is really expensive, then she will add that to the price of the project.

Therefore, the price for the images selected above may be much less than $170; in fact it might be $0 because it is rolled into the price of the book layout job.

Don't Buy Too Soon

I have talked about the process of finding and buying images. However, I would recommend that you do not buy the images yourself. The iStockphoto web site will allow you to download a free version of each image that you are interested in. You can place this in your manuscript while you are working. You will also find that the image has a visible watermark to prevent you from going to final press with the free version.

As you select the images to be used in your book you load them into a "Lightbox." This is just a folder at iStockphoto where you can collect all of the images that you are interested in. You can then share that Lightbox with your layout artist and let them do the licensing.

This is a much better approach that buying pictures yourself and then finding that they are not quite right when you start mixing them together and placing them in the book format. You really need to see how everything looks together before you make a decision about which images to license. Your layout artist is a talented professional and will probably have a number of suggestions to improve the visual appeal of your work. They might suggest a better set of images than those you have selected.

For one of my books I found a photo that perfectly conveyed the key idea in one of the chapters. I was very eager to have this included in the book. But I had not looked at the price. My layout artist noticed that the image licensed for almost 150 credits, or over $200. She found an alternate image that was not quite as perfect, but which licensed for only 10 credits. We both agreed that saving $200 in image licensing was the right decision.

For a book entitled *Fortune Cookies* the artist and I reviewed hundreds of stock photos of Chinese fortune cookies. We changed our minds repeatedly on which four images to license until we finally settled on a set that we felt worked well together throughout the book. We did all of this work using the free versions and then paid only for the images that we finally selected.

You may find some great images in your early searches of iStockphoto. But do not license anything until you are certain that it will be part of your final product.

Money	Time
$0 right now, but perhaps $50 later in the process.	1 day spread over several weeks of using iStockphoto.

PART II

Publishing

Where the writing rubber meets the publishing road.

Chapter 5

Hiring Help

You are not going to be able to do absolutely every job in the publishing process yourself. At some point you have to admit that you are the author with the story and the talent for putting that story into words. But you do not have the right skills to create all of the document formats, graphic designs, labeling, and marketing that make up a printed book.

This is where you hire help. This is where you start to spend that $1,000 budget we talked about earlier.

The internet makes finding, hiring, and managing professional help much easier than it used to be. There are several companies that have created a portal to bring together customers like you with talented contractors who can help you. These portals allow you to find and hire talent from anywhere in the world.

You do not have to Google the entire internet and hope that you find an individual or a firm that can handle your book layout. You do not have to worry about strange contractors stealing your money or your manuscript. You can hire talent through an organized marketplace that knows how to protect the interests of both parties involved in a deal.

Talent Portals

I have been very happy with the talent that I have found through the Elance® marketplace. This is a web site that brings together the freelance contractors who have special expertise, with the businesses and authors that need their help. Imagine a web site similar to eBay®, but offering services instead of products. Elance contains the same buyer protections that eBay is well known for. It is structured to protect the interests of both the contractors and the customers hiring them.

> **Freelance Talent Portals:**
> Elance®—http://www.elance.com/
> iFreelance®—http://www.ifreelance.com/
> Project4Hire®—http://www.project4hire.com/

I have used Elance for a couple of dozen jobs, including twelve book layout projects. Because I am so familiar with their services and happy with the results, I recommend that you use them as well.

On your first visit to the Elance.com web site, select "Register." Because you are trying to hire talent, you will then select "Create Your Account".

The registration process is free. It requires that you select a method for paying for the services you will be hiring. But there is no cost until you actually hire someone to work for you.

Elance manages the exchange of information and money between the customer and the contractor. You make payment to Elance and they in turn pay the person that you have hired. They serve as an intermediary in the transaction just as eBay® and Amazon.com® do for people selling products. Your financial information is not shared with the providers that you hire.

Elance can also help you to settle any disputes that may arise with a vendor and can refund your money if necessary.

As with most commercial sites, there are several different methods for making payment to your contractors. You can pay with a credit card or a PayPal® account. Both are equally secure. My only recommendation is that, if you will make payments via PayPal, do not use the same user name and password for your Elance account that you use for your PayPal account.

Once you have an Elance account take some time to browse the site and look at the services that they have to offer. There are hundreds of unique services offered on the site, certainly more than you will ever be able to use. If you select the "Hire" option on the top menu bar you will see a list of some of the profiled service providers. Notice that the short summary shows you their special skills, their location, their typical rates, the number of customers they have had on Elance, and the feedback they have received from those customers. This is a lot of data in just a few lines.

If you click on one of these vendors you will get a more comprehensive profile of their services and past performance. Each provider usually posts samples of their work, which is very helpful in determining whether their style and previous work match your project.

There are so many providers on the site that it is almost impossible to select one by browsing through the list. If you select the category "Design and Multimedia" you will find that there are over 29,000 providers offering their services on the site. This is far too many for you to evaluate individually.

It is much better to start by putting your job up for bid. Instead of looking at individual providers, you post your job and specify the kind of talent that you need. The people who have that talent, the necessary tools, and the time to do the job will then find you. They will place a bid at the price they would like to be paid and the time it will take them to do it. You can then compare a number of bids and select the best one for your project. From this list of bids you will find someone who has the experience to do your job. You should read the feedback that they have received from previous customers to see if their customers were happy with their work.

Since this is your first posting on the site I would stress that you are looking for a vendor with a successful track record. Do not accept a very low priced offer from a provider who has no previous customers and no feedback on performance.

Book Layout Designer

A book designer will take your electronic manuscript and generate two PDF files. The first will contain the internal pages of the book. This will include any figures or photos that appear in the text and will look just like the inside of any book in your library. The second file is a wrap-around cover for the book. It will show the front cover, spine, and back cover all

Part II: Publishing

in one file. It will look like a paper book cover that has been carefully removed from the spine in one piece and laid flat on the table.

Once you have these two files you have what you need to move on to a printer who can turn those files into a printed book.

The book layout artist does a number of jobs that we take for granted when we read a book. They make the artistic determinations about what will appear on every page.

Take a minute to examine the open book in your hands right now.

How do you like the style and size of the text font? Where are the page numbers positioned? Is there a decorator around the page number or a footer? What header do you see on the top left and top right pages? How did the chapter header look? Did you like the large opening character that started the chapter? How was the opening title page designed?

These details give the inside of a book it character and flavor. You may not consciously notice of them, but they significantly influence your opinion of the book.

If you have included any figures, tables, graphics, or photos in the book, your designer will rework these so that they fit the style of the printed page. He or she will also insure that they are in a format that will be perfect when it comes off of the printing press.

These details make each book a visually appealing product. You are looking for a designer who has done all of this before. Examine each bidder's portfolio for previous work that you would be proud to put your own name on.

Posting Your First Job

Posting a job on Elance is relatively simple. Select "Hire" and then "Post Job" from the menu across the top. The system will present you with a form to complete.

Job Title

Select a title that is short and descriptive. Perhaps, "Detective Novel Layout" or "Book: Managing Sewer Workers" or "Hardcover on Discrete Mathematics"

This should be something that describes both the format and the content of the project. Keep in mind that you are competing with other customers who are trying to attract the best talent as well. The bidders should be able to see that this is a book project rather than just a marketing brochure or conference program.

Category and Subcategory

Identifying the category will really narrow down the set of providers who know how to handle a book. Select "Design & Multimedia". Then under subcategory select "Page & Book Design". This targets the providers who want to work on a project like yours.

Job Description

In the job description box write a short two, three, or four paragraph summary of what you want done. Notice that to the right of the entry box there is a link to "See a sample job description." Definitely use this to see what Elance recommends. Their ideas will get you thinking along the right line.

Elance offers a template for the details that you should include in your posting. Use it. They also offer a link to existing jobs similar to yours. This will let you see the descriptions that other people have used. Read a couple of these postings to get a feel for an effective job description.

The points that I usually try to make in my posting are:
1. Specify that the project is for a book layout and design,
2. Give the number of pages and chapters in the manuscript,
3. Give an estimate of the number of figures, tables, and graphics,
4. Specify the language that the book is written in, and
5. Estimate the time you expect the project to take. Three weeks is typical.

Hiring Help

There are several additional items that you might include to zero in on someone who has done work very similar to yours.

6. Binding type of the book. For this $1,000 project we envision a book that is "perfect bound" on crème paper.
7. Size of the book. Typical sizes are 5" x 8", 5.5" x 8.5", or 6" x 9".
8. Printer to be used is Lightning Source Inc. at http://www.lightningsource.com/

We will describe details about these last three items in later chapters. A book that is perfect bound on crème paper, 5.5" x 8.5" to be printed by Lightning Source is very specific. It is also exactly what I recommend for your first book.

Letting the bidders know that you are printing with a specific company is very helpful. Many of them have experience preparing files for those companies and can mention this in their bids. It also allows them to check the specific requirements of that printer before entering a bid. Since you specified the printer, you are expecting finished files that can be uploaded to that printer and will be successfully processed into a paper book. If the files that they deliver do not meet this specification, then you have legitimate grounds to ask them to rework the files or to provide a refund.

Your book designer will be working with several services on the Lightning Source web site. It helps if they have done this before and can deliver files that work perfectly with this printer's systems.

Desired Skills

This part for the form is primarily a list of all of the software programs that are used by "Page & Book Design" professionals. There are also a couple of personal skills in the list. You might select the following options:

- Cover Design
- Graphic Design
- InDesign
- Illustrator

The first two are the skills of the contractor. The last two are software programs. You might also include proficiency other software packages. My opinion is that you just need to select a sample of skills and tools that illustrate the talent that is required. The contractor is the expert in these tools and will know which are compatible with your job and with the process enforced by the Lightning Source printer.

Job Type

You can elect to pay your designer by the hour or by the job. I recommend selecting "Fixed Price" and then setting the price in the "$50 to $500" range. The layout of your first book should fall under $500. If you have a lot of graphics, then it might cost all of $500. But I do not recommend accepting a bid larger than this unless there is some reason that your job is particularly complicated. In most cases, the page length of the book has very little impact on the cost to do the layout. Once the interior page style is created, the software automatically applies it to the entire manuscript.

Note that some bidders will offer a price over $500. They take the "$50 to $500" category as a guideline, but are not forced to bid in that range if they think it is a larger job.

Job Location
You can specify the country, city, or zip code that you want the vendor to live and work in. I contend that in the 21st century there is no reason that your job has to be done in your home state or in New York City, the book capital of the world. You should select "No Preference" and accept bids from anywhere in the world.

Though I leave my jobs open to anyone in the world, I do not believe that every country has the talent to do every job well. Through my own trial and error I have learned that it is difficult to work with people from distinctly different cultures. You and they have grown up in completely different environments. They may have different working days and holidays. They may have different meanings for the words "prompt" and "soon." Though you may both read and write the same language, it does not mean that you both have the same understanding of that language.

I have had excellent experience hiring vendors from the United States, Canada, England, Italy, and Panama. These providers all seemed to understand what I was looking for and what I meant when I asked for corrections to draft work. They were also generally on the same work schedule that I was accustomed to. Monday through Friday were work days, while Saturday and Sunday were not expected.

I have been less successful in hiring vendors from some other cultures. A web designer that I hired from India worked very hard and returned products quickly. But when I asked for changes he simply did not understand the idea of improving on his work. Later drafts were essentially the same as the first draft. It felt like we were going in circles around his original design. My descriptions of what I wanted never caused him to go off in a new, and in my opinion, better direction. In the end I had to tell him that this was not working and I wanted to cancel the project. I had paid him 50% of the agreed upon fee and felt that he had certainly worked hard enough to keep this payment. However, he insisted that if I was not happy, then he wanted to refund all of my money. It was very important to him that his feedback on Elance reflected that he treated all of his customers fairly.

Continue

That is it. You have described your job and are ready to post it to the Elance community for bidding. Click "continue" to wrap up the project.

Featured Project

The last question that you have to answer is whether you want this job to be "Featured" in Elance. This means that it will be posted higher up in the list of the open jobs that the contractors search through. This provides additional advertising so your project will attract the best vendors. This service costs $15. Since posting a job on Elance is completely free, there are dozens or hundreds of jobs posted to the site that are never awarded. They might come from an employer like you who is just trying to see how many vendors are available for a job. Or maybe one contractor is trying to see the prices that his competitors are charging. By paying $15 to be Featured you demonstrate that you are serious about this posting. You have spent $15 to bring attention to your job, while many of the other postings have not spent anything at all.

If I am going to evaluate a number of bids, I want to make sure that the best bids in my price range are available to choose from. I do not want the best providers to miss my posting because it was buried in the long list of jobs that were posted that day.

Evaluations

Once you post your job you will begin receiving bids from providers all over the world. Most of these will arrive within two days of the posting. My experience is that some come within the hour. You will receive an email from Elance when bidders appear and you can return to your Elance account to review them.

As you look at all of the services that are offered, I would recommend using the following evaluation criteria:

1. *Price.* You will receive bids over the $500 maximum that you specified. I do not think that a simple perfect bound book design should cost more than $500. I would decline any bids over $500. Look for a bid closer to $400.
2. *Time.* Decline any bids that will take longer than four weeks.
3. *Country.* Select a provider who is in a country that has a similar culture to your own, for the reasons described above.
4. *Portfolio and Attachments.* Look for someone who has done a job similar to yours and whose work you really like.
5. *Feedback.* Evaluate the feedback and the ratings that have been given by previous customers. Look for a rating that is at least 4.0 and preferably higher than 4.5. Keep in mind this it is almost impossible to get a 5.0 when averaging evaluations from many projects. But also expect that customers tend to inflate scores because to be nice to the contractor when a project has been successful. Also, if a contractor receives several really bad scores they will probably abandon their account and create a new one to start fresh.
6. *Proposal Text.* Read the personal response from the provider for your job. Does it sound like a form letter or did they write it specifically to you? Does this person have any special talents or experience that makes them perfect for your job?
7. *Roll the Dice.* I have often received two or three proposals that appear equally good. It can be difficult to determine

which is the best bid for your job. In this case you have to go with your hunches. What feels the best? I never make this decision based on the lowest price. Since I have a budget of $500 for the design, I am happy to spend up to that amount to get the best person for the job. I am never interested in saving $100 or $200 on the design. This design will affect the entire quality of the book.

Award

Once you have selected a provider, the Elance system is going to ask you to take two more steps to get the project started. First, you have to set milestones for the project, then fund those milestones.

Milestones

A milestone is a specific task that has to be accomplished in order to make progress toward the finished book. The whole project is completed by completing a series of milestones on time. As the hiring agent, you are allowed to set the milestones for the project and assign the amount that you will pay to the provider when he or she accomplishes each milestone. The Elance system then allows the provider to suggest changes to those milestones if they do not agree with the schedule or the amount of payment.

As an experienced project manager I am very familiar with the concept of moving forward via milestones. I also understand something about the importance of structuring these so that the provider is motivated to work on the project diligently and to finish it on time.

Funding

Your milestones should start with smaller payments for smaller tasks and proceed toward larger payments at the end. You should always reserve a significant payment for the very last milestone called "Final Delivery". The Elance system is structured so that you will not get cheated out of your money. But you need to make sure the provider is motivated to work all the way to the end. That is why you put a significant payment at the end of the project.

For a $400 book layout project I have had great success using the following milestones:

Milestone	Payment	Due Date
Draft Cover	$100	End of First Week
Complete Interior	$150	End of Second Week
Final Book	$150	End of Third Week

You will notice that I do not have a milestone for "Finished Cover". Typically, I work with the designer on several different drafts until we reach something that I am almost completely happy with. At that point I pay for the "Draft Cover" milestone and we move on to the interior. But I have found that once the interior is completed and the final wrap-around version of the cover is delivered that I always have a few last minute changes to the cover. My designer has been very easy to work with on these changes and I have never felt the need to hold onto some money specifically to cover these changes.

Most designers will promise to work with you until you are satisfied with the final product. My designer has been true to this and we have always finished every project happily. In most cases the product I get back is better than I had expected (thank you Adina).

If you can follow these instructions you will have hired a designer for your book and begun the process of working together. Hopefully it will go brilliantly and you will be very happy with the person you choose. Of course, there is no guarantee, nor a magic formula that always leads to the best choice. But I think you will be able to find someone who is as eager and as professional as you are.

Money	Time
$15 for premium posting.	2 days for bids, 1 day for closing the deal.

Chapter 6

100% Proof

All writers think they are masters of the English language and amazing artistes at crafting the text that appears in their books. But writing is like hearing your own spoken voice, it sounds completely different in your head than it does on paper. Because you know what you are trying to say, your brain helps to make sense of the words on the page. What is actually written is very different from what you hear when you read your own writing.

We all need the assistance of an outside reader to determine whether our words are working. Does it carry the message that we intended? Is it even intelligible? Does it evoke the right emotion? Is it grammatically consistent? Word processors have marvelous spell checking tools and moderate grammar checking tools. But the grammar tools are far too primitive to help with the deep content of a book. Only the human mind can do that.

Your editor, proof reader, or ghost writer may be your spouse, sibling, or best friend. You may have someone close to you with the talent and the time to improve your writing. If so, then you are blessed. You should allow this person to help and you should reward them with appreciation, dinner, small gifts, and money.

Editors

If you do not have someone to help you, you will have to hire professional help. There are hundreds of people eager to accept work as an editor, proof reader, or ghost writer. You can find a few thousand of them on Elance. The process for discovering the good ones is the same as that described for layout designers in the previous chapter. Create a project and put it up for bid. Within a few days you will have offers from eight to ten editors from all over the world.

Most editors or proofreaders want to know two things about your job before they give you a price. First, how many words is it? They typically provide their services "by the word" so you are going to have to use the word processor to count the words in the document and include that in your bid posting.

Second, what language is the document written in? Given that you are reading this book in English and following my instructions to get to the English version of Elance, you are probably writing for an English speaking audience. But this should be explicitly stated in your project description.

Ghost Writers

An editor is trying to fix the words and phrases that you have already created. But, a ghost writer will help you create some of the text itself. You may provide them an outline, references to resources, first drafts, or roughly scribbled ideas.

You can hire a ghost writer to do editing work as well. For one of my books I needed help finishing several chapters. I hired a ghost writer to work on the chapters that I had written and to write big portions of the last four chapters that I had only drafted crudely. Stanley charged me about the same price that I had paid editors in the past. He also took it upon himself to clean up all of my text. So I ended up getting both editing and ghost writing services for one package price (thank you Stanley).

This was an unusual situation. Generally you should expect to pay more for ghost writing services than for editing services.

Evaluations

The evaluation process that I have used for editors and ghost writers is almost the same as that for book layout jobs.

1. *Price.* The highest price that you should pay for editing is one cent per word. This is almost a standard rate among experienced editors. The lowest credible rate I have received is 2/3 of a cent per word, or about $300 for a 50,000 word book.

2. *Time.* Editing a typical 100 to 150 page book should take between one and two weeks. But it can be longer if the editor is working on other projects at the same time.

3. *Native English Speaker.* Every language in the world is unique and complicated. We all spend decades learn-

ing to speak it, read it, and write it. Your editor should be a native speaker of the language you are using. The language of the book cannot be their second language because they will not get the grammar right, no matter how long they have been speaking or reading it as a second language.

4. *Experience and Education.* Look at the providers qualifications. What suggests that they know the English language better than you do? Have they worked for a publisher? Do they have a degree in English, Writing, or Literature? Have they written their own books? Your editor should be more experienced at this than you are.

5. *Feedback.* Look at the feedback and the ratings they have received from previous customers. I like a rating that is at least 4.0 and preferably higher than 4.5. Keep in mind this it is almost impossible to get a 5.0 when averaging ratings from many customers. But also know that customers tend to give slightly higher scores to be nice when a project has been successful. Also, if a provider receives several really poor scores they will probably abandon that account and create a new account to start fresh.

6. *Proposal Text.* Read the proposal text. Does this text sound like someone who is proficient enough to edit your entire book?

7. *Roll the Dice.* If you cannot decide between two or three offers, go with your hunches.

For one project I hired a young woman who was living in Medicine Hat, Alberta, Canada. She was clearly a native English speaker and had published a couple of her own books. She had been through an editing and proofreading certificate program with a local college and had a number of very good reviews of her work. She charged me 2/3 of a cent per word and did an excellent job. Stacey was one of my hunches.

100% Proof

As good as these editors are they are not going to bring your book to the 100% level for printing. They will get it into the "90% Plus" area. But it is still your job to go through it again and make sure it is telling your story. You will always find a few remaining grammatical errors. But your final read is meant to make sure the story flows so that your message is getting through.

Once you and the editor have been through it that last time, it is finished. It is time to print. Certainly, you can always improve it. But at some point you have to stop changing your book and move forward. If you strive for absolute perfection you may never let yourself finish.

The Mathematics of Editing

Dr. George Polya, a famous mathematician at Stanford University, has demonstrated an equation for figuring out how many errors remain in the manuscript of a book. It requires sending a copy of the manuscript to two editors for independent proof reading. Let's call these editors Andy and Bethany. When each returns their manuscript, count the errors they found - A for Andy and B for Bethany. Then compare the two sets of errors to figure out how many of the errors are Common to both lists, call it C. Common means that Andy and Bethany found the same error.

With just that information you can estimate the number of errors that were in the original manuscript and how many still remain hidden in the corrected manuscript. First, calculate the estimated total number of errors (T) that were in the manuscript that you sent to Andy and Bethany.

$$T = (A * B)/C$$

If Andy found 100 errors, Bethany found 120 errors, and these lists had 90 errors in common, then the total estimate is:

$$T = (100 * 120)/90 = 133 \text{ errors.}$$

The next step is to figure out how many are still remaining (R) in the manuscript. That is:

$$R = T - (A + B - C)$$
$$R = 133 - (100 + 120 - 90) = 133 - 130 = 3$$

The point of this mathematic exercise is to illustrate that there are almost always more errors hidden in your manuscript than you can find. Only when two editors return the same number of errors, and they are exactly the same set of errors, can you feel confident that all of the errors are gone from your manuscript.

You should be a little comforted to know that a few errors remain in all published books.

Money	Time
$300 or about 2/3 of a cent per word.	2 weeks.

Chapter 7

Great Designs

Once you have awarded the book design contract you are going to become very close with your designer. He or she is going to try to capture the style and feel that you had in mind for your book. Remember that they have not known you very long. They have no idea what you have been writing, thinking, and dreaming about for months or years. They are also not a proofreader. They usually don't read the text of the book to feel of the content. They rely on what you tell them.

Be Available

The design process can be accomplished in three weeks if both of you stick to the job. But if one of you wanders off on another project, it can be delayed for weeks. You should be able to check your email and check your Elance account for updates every day. When your designer sends you the first draft of your book cover, you should be around to download it that same day.

Once you have the drafts, you should be diligent about reviewing them and getting back to your designer within a day, two at the most. If you are going to make it through a couple of draft covers in a week, then you have to be able to respond to each draft within a day. The same goes for drafts of the interior.

Give Guidance

Your designer is going to start with the style of cover that they are accustomed to. It will be their style, not your style. If you want them to think like you, then you have to share your ideas with them. Describe the cover that you imagine. Send them samples of covers and interiors that you would like to mimic. Some of these samples are available on Amazon.com.

Use "feeling" words in your descriptions. Your designer is an artistic person. They will understand what you mean if you say you want something "sharper", "louder", "warmer", or "more Chinese". Remember the discussion about hiring someone from a similar culture? This is one of the reasons for that—so you both understand what instructions like "louder" means.

Listen

You hired a professional book designer. They have more experience creating books than you do. When their ideas are going in a different direction, listen to them. Try to imagine what they have in mind. You want their ideas work for you, as well as their hands.

For my book *Fortune Cookies: Small secrets on how to make a fortune*, I asked for the cover to "look more Chinese." I suggested adding an image of a Chinese dragon or a paper lantern. My designer tried these, but also commented that the images did not seem to work well with the cover design. She suggested that "more Chinese" could be accomplished by simply using red text for the title and the wording on the cover. This simple change was excellent and gave it just the flavor it needed.

It is much easier to agree on the layout of the interior pages because there are fewer options. You are usually just deciding on the font, header, and page numbering; along with a few simple decorators. Interior style changes can be resolved much faster than cover changes.

Proofread

When you receive the drafts of the cover and the interior, you must proofread every word very carefully. Typographical errors sneak into every page and it is almost impossible to find them all. Even the most meticulously prepared book from the best publishing house ships with a few errorrs still inside.

When your drafts come back to you, they will have a different layout and placement of the text on the page. These subtle shifts will allow your mind to see the page differently. It will reveal errors that you could not see in earlier versions.

When I am proof reading I typically open another text document and list every error with a single line like this:

p.4 first para—change "As a result, most people assume" to "As a result, most people believe"
p.27—Lighten or brighten the picture of Edison just a little more.
p.178—Put the bulleted list into a shaded text box.

I try to be as clear as possible so the designer can quickly find each error.

Proofread every word of every draft that comes to you. Each draft is one more opportunity to find and remove a hidden mistake. When the entire interior layout arrives this proofreading is going to take some time. But you only have one chance to do it. It is too late once you move into the printing process.

Get the Cover Right

The text, colors, fonts, and images on the cover should all say that this is an original and exciting book. Do not accept a book cover that looks like it belongs to a very fast, easy to create, self-published book. You want it to be as professional and distinct as possible given the talent that you have hired.

Look at many book covers for ideas that you want to use on your own cover. A book designer has the ability to create thousands of different styles. You just need to show them where to go.

A final note, book layout designers are not usually illustrators. They cannot draw new, original, and custom images by hand. Creating a custom illustration for the cover is typically not part of their bid to you. You can expect them to use stock photos and illustrations along with unique fonts and colors. If you want a custom illustration, that will require another job posting on Elance.

Money	Time
$400.	3 weeks.

Chapter 8

Take a Number

Most writers and self-publishers are intimidated by the International Standard Book Number and its more alien cousin, the bar code. These seem like something reserved for big corporate printing houses and beyond the reach of a small publisher.

Actually, both of these are easy to purchase. Everyone gets their ISBNs from the same source. Bowker® Inc. manages, distributes, and sells these numbers to the entire book publishing industry. You can buy a single ISBN or a larger block of ten on their web site.

http://www.myidentifiers.com/

The site contains a great deal of information on ISBN's and other identifiers. But for this job, you just need to make a purchase. You can choose between a single ISBN for $125 or a block of 10 for $250.

Which is right for you?

Let's try a shopping analogy. If you were shopping for a single pair of shoes and found that the store was having a gigantic "10 pair for the price of 2!" sale, what would you do? Would you purchase just one pair of shoes as you had planned? Or would you shop around and find a second pair that you can really use? Just one more pair and you can have eight for free. I think everyone would pay for two pair and come away with ten. That is what I would recommend for your ISBNs as well. As soon as you finish publishing your first book, you are going to be eager to do another one. You might as well get the best deal on your ISBNs right up front.

On the web site you will find the blocks of ISBNs listed under "ISBN Packages", then select "ISBN Blocks" in the submenu.

13 Digits vs. 10 Digits

The current standard is a 13 digits ISBN. However, in the past, the standard was just 10 digits. MyIdentifiers.com just sells the 13 digit ISBN, though most books include the older 10 digit number as well. You do not have to buy or track that 10 digit number. Your book designer will work with the printing company to auto-generate the 10 digit number that corresponds to your 13 digit ISBN. You do not have to worry about this.

Bar Codes for Free

Bowker also sells the bar code containing the ISBN. But, you do not have to pay for this. A finished bar code on the back of a book contains two essential pieces of information - the ISBN and the retail price. You cannot know what the retail price is at this point. Neither can you guess at the price to go with all 10 of the ISBNs that you receive in a block.

Your book designer will be using a tool on the Lightning Source printer's web site to generate this two-part bar code—

and it does not cost anything. Bar code creation is part of the package that is included in book design and it is a free service offered by Lightning Source to attract designers and publishers.

Once you have purchased the ISBN for a book you just have to provide it to your designer to be included on the copyright page, back cover, and bar code. You will also enter it into the Lightning Source web site when you start your printing project. From there, the ISBN will be carried through the entire publishing world by the databases that exchange this information.

Description of the ISBN from the Bowker® web site

"The International Standard Book Number (ISBN) is a 13-digit number that uniquely identifies books and book-like products published internationally, allowing for more efficient marketing of products by booksellers, libraries, universities, wholesalers and distributors. The ISBN Agency assigns ISBNs at the direct request of publishers, e-book publishers, audio cassette and video producers, software producers and museums and associations with publishing programs. Bowker is the Official ISBN Agency for the United States. The ISBN will establish and identify one title or edition of a title from one specific publisher and is unique to that edition. The ISBN, coupled with a descriptive meta-data record, ensures that information needed to make a level purchasing decision is communicated to the consumer accurately and reliably, particularly in cases where the same product or format is available for purchase on multiple channels. In the digital supply chain, most major search engines, e-tailers, library web sites, social network applications, mobile phones and other entities cataloging information about books continue to leverage the ISBN as a cataloging mechanism and to search-optimize such information for consumer discovery.

Money	Time
$25 each, when you buy a block of 10 for $250.	1 day.

Chapter 9

Finding Gutenberg

Your manuscript is ready to print. It has been written, edited, and formatted. There are many print-on-demand companies that can help you with the next step. Each has a slightly different set of services and printing agreements.

I am going to point you toward the printer that I use and have been very successful with.

Lightning Source

Lightning Source® Inc. (http://www.lightningsource.com/) offers all of the printing services that you will need to finish your book. They also provide promotional services that are worth their weight in gold. They are primarily a printing company, not a full service publisher, which means that they do not want to own your book. They just want to help you get it into print.

The LSI web site provides services that will help your book designer create digital files that are ready for the printing process. One of these creates a bar code from your ISBN and book price. Another will deliver a perfectly measured template for the spine cover of your book. Tools like these make the book designer's life easier by eliminating disparities that often arise when the files are transferred to the printer.

I started using Lightning Source because my first book designer recommended them. She had worked with several companies and felt that LSI had the best services and the best tools to help her do her job. Because she was familiar with LSI, it reduced the amount of work that both of us had to do.

I looked at several of the print-on-demand companies and found that some wanted to assume the role of publisher. They expected exclusive agreements on printing and distributing my books. And they wanted to take a large amount of the profit from each sale. This is not what I was looking for and not what I recommend for you.

With LSI all ownership and royalties belong to you. That is the model I recommend.

Ingram Catalog

LSI offers a promotional service through which the listing of your book is passed on to Ingram Publishers for inclusion in their catalog for distributors and book buyers. The fee for this service is extremely reasonable at $60. This covers a one-time entry with the book's summary, cover image, price, and publisher's information.

Finally, LSI can make your book available in both the US and the UK. The services for UK distribution are almost identical to that for the US. It will result in your book being available in British Pounds and listed with UK online bookstores.

Web Site Registration

As with every online service provider, the first step at Lightning Source is to create an account and provide a method of payment. When you begin the registration process, LSI will ask if you are a publisher or not. Using the model described in this book, you <u>are</u> a publisher. You are playing the role of both author and publisher.

What is the name of your publishing company?

You should create a unique name for your publishing company. This is the name and address that will appear on the copyright page of the book and in all electronic catalogs. You are not the first author to self-publish. Walt Whitman famously self-published *Leaves of Grass*. James Redfield self-published *The Celestine Prophecy*. Richard Bolles self-published *What Color is Your Parachute?* Jack Canfield self-published *Chicken Soup for the Soul*. Thousands of authors have used this approach to get their work into print.

I would recommend that you create a unique publishing company name and use a post office box as the address. However, there is no reason that you cannot use your name for this, as in "Roger Smith Press" and your home address. But, more about that later.

Once you have completed the registration process you are ready to begin submitting titles to be printed.

Submitting a Print Job

Submitting your first print job can be a little confusing. Before you get started you need to have the following information ready:

1. *Cover File.* PDF or other acceptable file format for the cover of the book.
2. *Interior File.* PDF or other file format containing all of the internal pages of the book.
3. *ISBN.* The 13-digit ISBN that you purchased from Bowker's MyIdentifiers.com web site.
4. *Title and Subtitle* of your book.
5. *Book Summary.* A description of the book that you want to appear at Amazon.com and other online bookstores. This is usually a version of the summary that you put on the back cover of the book.
6. *Subject Categories.* Ideas for three subject categories that cover your book. Imagine that these are the shelves of a bookstore where your book would be located. LSI has a list of subject categories that you will choose from that is derived from the "BISAC Subject Headings" catalog that we described earlier.

To begin, select "My Library" from the tool bar, then "Set Up New Title".

You can choose to make this book available to all distributors and bookstores, or you can choose to limit it to your own private orders. The latter is usually for books about personal family history, a diary to be passed on to relatives, and similar topics that are for private distribution. However, most authors will want to select "Title for Full Distribution Services".

If you have prepared a version of the book for the Microsoft, Adobe, or Palm electronic reader programs, then you can select these as well. Note that publishing your book for distribution on the Amazon® Kindle or the Barnes & Noble Nook™ requires that you submit those directly through Amazon or B&N. That is why they are not options on this form.

Most of the title setup is done through the form shown in Figure 9-1.

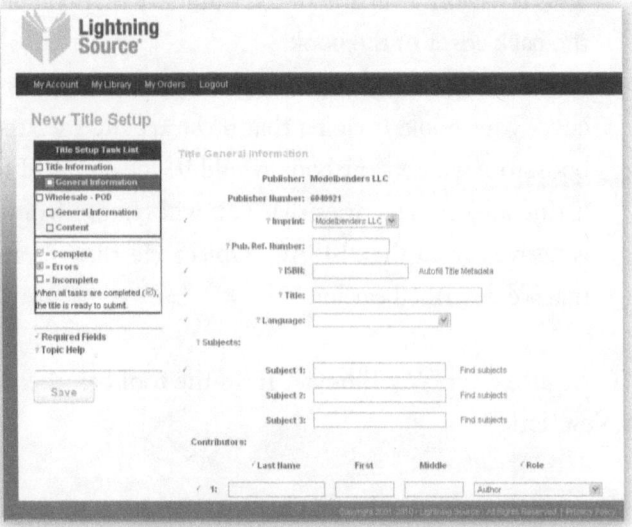

Figure 9-1. Lightning Source Title Setup Screen

Notice that at the top of this form, the name of the publisher is already loaded. This comes from the information that you entered during the account registration process.

"Pub. Ref. Number" is an optional field that allows you to assign this book a number or code that you are using for your own personal tracking of the title. Some authors simply number their books 1, 2, 3, etc. Others create some contraction of the title and a number. This field is completely optional.

"ISBN" is for the 13-digit ISBN without any dashes.

"Title" calls for the full title of the book. This includes your preferred capitalization, punctuation, and subtitle. This is how the book will be listed in online bookstores.

"Language" in which the book is written.

Subjects. Use the LSI forms to select three standard subject categories for your book. When you click on "Find Subjects" you will receive a form that allows you to enter a keyword and search of all entries in the subject catalog. After experimenting with this search you will be amazed at the large number and variety of subjects that are used to categorize books. It will take a little trial-and-error to locate three appropriate subject listings for your book.

"Contributors" calls for you to identify all of the people who have made a contribution to this book. The first is clearly the

author. But there are many additional forms of contribution that you can identify here. Look through the "Role" field on the right side to see if any of the others apply to your work.

"Publication Date" is the date on which you want to consider this book published. You may back date this or you may choose to use the date on which you are setting up the title.

"List Price" is the retail price that appears in the bar code. Note that LSI checks the price you enter in this field with that in the bar code. If they do not match, they will bounce your title back to you for correction.

Wholesale Discount. Book distributors and online stores like Amazon.com will be buying their books directly from Lightning Source. Clearly they do not pay the full retail price because it would not give them any room to make a profit. You determine the price that they will pay using this field. It is customary for a distributor or large book buyer to receive their titles at a 55% discount to the retail price, though you may set this at any level you like. I have found that if you set this discount less than 55% the online book stores will assign your book a higher shipping fee to make up the difference. To compensate for this discount, it is important that you set the full retail price of the book approximately three times the production costs for each copy. This will allow you to make a profit after giving Amazon.com a 55% discount. More details on production cost are described later in this chapter.

Returnable. All books that are stocked in a commercial bookstore are considered returnable to the publisher. Those that are not sold are either shipped back to the publisher or destroyed. But in both cases, the bookstore receives a full refund for the books that they did not sell. As a small publisher you may not be able to afford to take this chance. If you are not willing to refund all unsold copies, then you should set this field to "No." Note that unsold copies are shipped back to the publisher, not to the printing company. You are the publisher. That means they will come back to the address that you entered when you registered with LSI—your home address or your Post Office box.

Selecting the Paper

From the beginning of this book we have been targeting a specific type, size, and paper for your first book. There are many options to choose from. But my goal was to make the process as simple as possible your first time through. I recognize that you may have very different ideas for what your first book should look like. The size of the book was determined back when you gave directions to your book layout designer. The cover was also largely set at that time. Those choices allowed the designer to create the digital files that you are now bringing to LSI. The type of paper that it is printed on is important because it determines how thick the interior of the book is. This determines how wide the spine will be.

To walk you through the process, I am recommending the following specifications for your book:

- Perfect Bound
- 5.5" x 8.5"
- Crème paper

You are about to enter this information into the LSI web form which results in the creation your first proof copy. The LSI web site gives a larger number of options for the size, style, and paper for your book. I have always chosen to publish my books in one of the common tradebook sizes—5" x 8"; 5.5" x 8.5"; or 6" x 9". Most of my books have been on crème paper, which is a little thicker and heavier, ideal for smaller books.

Typically the cover of your book will be in color and the interior will be black and white.

Uploading Book Files

Once you have entered all of the data about your book, the LSI web site appears to be finished. But you are not done yet. You have entered a lot of data about your book into the forms, but you have not uploaded the PDF files that contain the contents of your book. The web site provides you with three options for delivering your book files to the printer. Since we are in the 21st century, I recommend that you upload your book files (cover and interior) directly from your computer. You eliminate the shipping and handling costs for CDs or DVDs, and the printing process will begin much sooner.

The LSI web site goes through a separate cycle for uploading and releasing the cover file and the interior file. Be sure that you do it twice, once for each part of the book. This part of their web site could use some improvement to make it more intuitive and user-friendly.

Once uploaded, the book is available for printing. It will take a day or two for LSI to confirm that the files you uploaded are compatible with their computerized printing system. If there is a problem with the files, they will notify you. In one case, my designer had used too much density of color in the cover image. That means it required more ink per inch than the LSI printing system could reproduce on paper. So they sent me an error message which was completely unintelligible to me. But I passed it on to the book designer and she knew exactly what the problem was. She fixed the color density and sent me a new version of the file. This is another reason to choose a book designer that is familiar with the requirements of your specific printer.

Proof Copy

Once all file formatting errors are fixed, you have the option to order a proof copy of the book to review before going into full production. The cost for this copy is $30 and it will take about 5 days to receive in the mail. I highly recommend ordering a proof copy to insure that everything went as you expected. The cost is very small, but it is a huge comfort to know what a book will look like when it is sold.

When you receive the proof copy, examine it carefully. Enjoy how good it feels to have created your first book. You are holding the first copy ever created of your very first book. If there are any mistakes in it, you will have to work with either LSI or your designer to fix them, and then order another proof copy. When the proof copy is good, you return to the LSI web site and select "Proof Acceptance." This lets them know that they can release the book into the distribution system for general purchase.

Congratulations

At this point you are effectively finished. You have produced a published book. The proof copy is the first instance of that book. It is time to celebrate. Take the time to enjoy what you have just accomplished.

You can now order your first case of books from LSI. The price of each book is determined by the number of pages. At this writing, the price is calculated as follows:

> **$0.90 for the cover**
> **$0.013 for each page.**

Therefore a single copy of a 110 page book would cost:

> **$0.90 + (110 * $0.013) = $2.33**

There are some additional costs to consider. LSI will charge you a $1.50 processing fee and about $22 for shipping. This means that you can have a case of 50 books for about $140.

> Case Cost to You = $2.33 x 50 books + $1.50 shipping + $22 shipping = $140

Calculating Retail Price

Loop back to the earlier question about what the retail price of the book should be. The retail price needs to be at least three times your production cost. So,

> Retail Price = $2.33 x 3 = $6.99

In the United States most book prices end in 95 cents. Therefore, you should choose to price the book at $6.95 or $7.95 if you plan to make any money. Using the standard 55% wholesale discount, this means that Amazon.com and other book sites will be purchasing the book from you for:

> Wholesale Price = $7.95 * 45% = $3.58
> (Math note: a 55% discount is the same as 45% of the retail price)

So your profit on the book will be about:

> Your Profit = $3.58 wholesale price - $2.33 production cost
> = $1.25 profit per book

Therefore, your profit percentage on the book is:

> **Profit Percentage = $1.25 / $7.95 = 15.7%**

When an author signs a contract with a big publishing company he or she often receives between 10% and 15% in royalties. Now that you see the costs associated with producing a book, you can understand why that is the range of their royalties.

Money	Time
$75 for Setup.	1 day for Setup.
$30 for Proof Copy.	5 days for Proof Copy.
$12 for Cataloging.	0 days for Cataloging.
$117 for Printing.	4 days for Printing.
$1 for Processing.	0 days for Processing.
$22 for Shipping.	6 days for Shipping.
Total = $257.	Total = 16 days.

Chapter 10

Talley Ho!

In a quick ten chapters we have covered everything from downloading a free word processor to ordering your first case of printed books. The essential details associated with the publication process were covered in Chapters 5 through 9. When you tally it all up, it looks like you have reached the finished product in much less than two months, and for a little more than $1,000. Success!

To be completely fair, you could have spent much more on the book. If your first book was 220 pages instead of the 110 that I use in the example, the cost of your first case of books would be almost double the $140 that I list below. A longer book would also cost twice as much in proof reading expenses, another $300. You might also have chosen a more expensive book designer, spending the full $500 that we budgeted.

But even if you double the size of the book and hire more expensive vendors, the price of production would go up only about $540 for a total of around $1,564.

You might also have worked on the project at a much more leisurely pace. Your book designer may have taken a few more days. You may not have been available to immediately review and approve the drafts. But even with those slips in the schedule, it is possible to get through the process in less than two months.

We live at a unique time in history. Never has it been possible to create a book so quickly and at such a reasonable price.

Competition in all areas of book production is increasing, which drives down costs. The process will just get faster and cheaper in the future. If you did it in two months for $1,000 today, you can do it faster and cheaper in the future.

Table 10-1.
Cost and Time Summary for Producing Your first Case of Books

Step	Cost	Time
Elance® Posting—Premium Fee (Chapter 5)	$15	1 day
Proof Reading (Chapter 6)	$300	14 days
Book Layout and Design (Chapter 7)	$400	21 days
ISBN Purchase (Chapter 8)	$25	1 day
Printing (Chapter 9)	$75 Setup $30 Proof Copy $12 Electronic Catalog $117 Printing $1 Processing $22 Shipping	1 day 5 days 0 days 4 day 0 days 6 days
Total	**$1,024**	**53 days**

You should sit back for a few moments and enjoy the fruits of your labor. Enjoy the rush that comes from creating the book that you always dreamed of. Congratulate yourself on being one of the few people in the world whose words are captured for generations of future readers. Use this accomplishment to brush aside some of the insecurities that you carry in your heart. If you can publish your own book, you are an exceptional individual and have the talent to do even more.

Share your accomplishment and your pride with other people. You have a case full of books. Start giving them to your family, coworkers, school friends, professional peers, and anyone else you can think of. Let them know what you have done.

PART III

Promoting

*Time to tell
the world.*

Chapter 11

You the Publisher

Part III: Promoting

Most of us got into self-publishing because we were authors with a burning need to release our work. As a result we generally consider publishing as a necessary sideline. Your new identity as a publisher may not seem to fit your personality or your professional goals. But once your book is printed you are both the publisher and the author. You must differentiate between playing each role. You are an author when you are writing and interact with readers. As author you are the person who is sharing your wisdom, expertise, and imagination with the public.

But when you are dealing with the printing company, distributors, and legal issues, you are acting as the publisher. You are the company that is representing the author and handling the business operations on their behalf.

It will take a few months to get used to this dual role. But it is no more complicated than the multiple roles that you already have in other parts of your life. You may be both an employee and a boss at work, both a husband and father at home, both a player and a coach on a softball team. Those are similar to what you will face as the newly anointed publisher of your own works.

Alternate Publishers

I have intentionally led you down the path toward self-publishing your book. There were at least two points along the way where you could have chosen a different path. Each would have led to using a third party to handle the publishing duties. First, I selected Lightning Source as the preferred printer because I wanted you to maintain ownership and responsibility for your books. You could have selected a number of other printers who expect you to let them be your publisher.

One of these publishers is Lulu®. If you visit the Lulu.com web site you will notice than in addition to providing a publishing service, they are also an online bookstore. Their books are available at Amazon.com and other online bookstores just as yours are, but they also use the Lulu.com web site.

You will find that publishers like Lulu.com offer a number of promotion packages for the books that they handle. These are all valuable, but they will not make a significant difference in the number of books that you sell. The book world is too inundated with new titles to pay much attention to any of these services. You are your own best promoter, or a close associate who is dedicated to your book. In a later chapter I will provide more details on ways to promote your book.

Alternate Services

The second fork in the path was where you created your account at Lightning Source. You had the choice to register as your own publisher or to access a list of publishing services for assistance. This would have led to services similar to that of Lulu.com. Both of these require that you release some ownership and control of your work, along with a significant portion of the profits.

But that is not the path that I chose to guide you through. The path in this book is just one of the hundreds of variations that are available in the publishing business. There are many web sites that you can visit to explore other alternatives.

> **Alternative Publishing Methods**
> **Lulu.com**
> **Smashwords.com**
> **FastPencil.com**
> **Scribd.com**
> **Xlibris.com**
> **iUniverse.com**
> **Blurb.com**
> **Amazon Digital Text Platform—**
> **http://www.dtp.amazon.com/**
> **Barnes & Noble PubIt™—**
> **http://www.barnesandnoble.com/pubit/index.asp**

Chapter 12

Promoted

On any given day, hundreds or even thousands of new books appear for the first time at Amazon.com. Yours will be one of the many that pop into existence on your publication date. But readers are not going to be notified about the great new author that has appeared on the scene unless you take steps to get your work noticed. Lightning Source provides two very easy and inexpensive services to start that promotion process.

LSI Digital Catalog

Lightning Source Inc. (LSI) maintains a digital catalog that is accessible to all online bookstores and that allows your book to appear in their databases. They charge a small fee of $12 per year to be included in this catalog.

The Digital Catalog fee is due at initial set up and each year thereafter for each title set up for wholesale, drop ship, and electronic ordering. The fee provides standardized BISAC subject coding with up to three subject categories. It also provides detailed title listings in all daily catalogs provided to US, UK and International distribution partners; a title summary; and a cover image.

BISAC subject coding is required for any title to be generally distributed. As the publisher you can remove a title from the Digital Catalog at anytime. If you discover incorrect title data displayed by any of LSI's distribution partners, LSI will confirm that correct title data is on file, and, if not, will correct their database and provide amended data to the distribution partner. LSI has no control over any distribution partner's erroneous display of data. They cannot guarantee that these partners will make corrections in their databases. But LSI will encourage the distribution partner to amend incorrect data.

Ingram Advance Catalog

Ingram Advance is a monthly catalog distributed to booksellers and libraries around the world. All titles submitted to LSI are eligible to be included in this catalog only once—specifically when they are first released from LSI. The fee for this is $60. With this marketing service, Ingram will include a short paragraph describing the title along with retail pricing information and a black & white cover image. As the publisher you may request that a title be advertised in *Ingram Advance* only at the time a title is submitted to Lightning Source for initial setup. Titles submitted to Ingram will appear in the catalog within three or four months after the title has been approved to print.

In my experience there is a slight peak in sales during the month in which the title appears in *Ingram Advance*. This indicates that book buyers are purchasing a few sample copies for consideration. The sales in following months will generally remain slightly higher than they were before the appearance in the catalog.

Both of these opportunities to promote your book are simple to trigger and inexpensive. They are essential, but not sufficient to create higher sales of your book.

Bookstore Appearances

No one is more interested in the success of your book than you are (and perhaps your mother). Therefore, you are the best promoter of your work. You can talk to bookstores about selling your book through a few local branches and providing space for a signing event. Large chains have some layers of bureaucracy to approve this, but they do have a process in place. If you can still find a small individually owned bookstore, they have a lot more discretion in allowing authors to promote books in their stores.

The most important factor in getting a signing event is your ability to convince the manager that your book is of interest to their customers. They know what sells at a location and they will be eager to bring in authors and titles that they think will attract customers. But if your title is on a topic that is foreign to them, you probably have slim chances of getting an appearance.

Radio Interviews

Local radio talk shows are always looking for guests. You can send a press release on your book to each local radio station and follow it up with a phone call. They are focused on a few specific topics that match the interests of their listeners. As a local media outlet they may also have an interest in local authors and local topics.

Radio talk shows are the local equivalent of appearing on the Oprah Winfrey Show®. They are engaged in an ongoing conversation with a dedicated audience. If you can add to that conversation then you may be a welcome guest.

Professional Groups

Professional associations are where you will find professional people who read professional books.

If your book is on a topic that appeals to a very unique profession, then it will be difficult to interest the local bookstore or radio station to invite you for an appearance. For these types of books you need to contact professional associations and trade magazines. You can offer to appear at their conferences, meetings, and luncheons to talk about your book and the expertise you have developed in writing it. You could purchase an advertisement in their newsletter. Or better yet, you could be interviewed for a column in the newsletter. Appearing in a column is better than buying an advertisement. First, it is free. Second, it carries a level of endorsement from the association.

Hiring Help

Not all writers are cut out to be promoters. If you have the patience to focus on a computer keyboard for hours, days, and weeks while writing a book, then you might not be able to turn on the charm necessary to attract the attention that a new book needs.

Even if you are an outgoing person, you may find it difficult to blatantly promote yourself and your own work. I am very aggressive in participating in my profession, but am very shy when talking about my own books. I was raised in a culture that discourages standing out in a crowd and bringing attention to yourself. That childhood programming inhibits my ability to promote my own books.

If this is the case for you, then you might need to return to Elance to hire a promoter. On the site you can search for "Public Relations" to find vendors who can help you with promotion. My experience has been that a PR professional will offer one of two services. For about $100 they will create and distribute a press release on your book. This is a simple one-time task to get your book started. For $1,000 or more they will design a PR campaign for the book and help you to begin executing that plan. This includes writing press materials, identifying associations, contacting radio stations, and distributing information to other media outlets.

Hope Is Not a Method

General Gordon Sullivan, the former Chief of Staff of the U.S. Army, wrote a book entitled *Hope is Not a Method*. By this unusual title, he meant that hope is no way to solve a problem. Hope does not overcome obstacles. Hope does not improve project schedules. Hope does not solve personnel issues. If a situation is going to get better, then you have to create a plan and take action.

Hope is not a method for promoting our book. You cannot rely on hope to get the attention of the reading public or the commercial book buyers. You have to create a plan and take action. If you do not, then your books will be lost in the ocean of new titles that are published every day. If you are just hoping that someone will notice your book, then you have the same chances as buying the winning lottery ticket—slim to none.

You have to build a plan and get started executing it if your book is going to be noticed. If you are not able to do it personally, then hire help. You need a voice in the market that is talking about your book.

Money	Time
$12 per year LSI Digital Catalog.	0 days.
$60 for Ingram Advance Catalog.	0 days.
$100 Press Release.	1 week.
$1,000 PR Campaign.	Several weeks.

Chapter 13

Untangling the Web

Part III: Promoting

Someone has said that, "If you are not online you do not exist." I would extend that to books as well. If your book does not have a web site it does not exist. A book is just like a person. It accumulates friends and fans. It has a life story to share. It offers advice and makes a contribution to the world. Your book needs to "be online." It needs to have a presence in the electronic world. This is where people will find the book. This is where they can find the author or the publisher. This is where they can chat with others who are interested in the book. This is where they can purchase another copy.

You are probably aware that all of the famous authors and some of their books have dedicated web sites, Facebook pages, and running blogs about the author's appearances. But you might have thought that such a presence for your book or your publishing company is too big of a step. You have already grown from a struggling author to a small publishing firm. How much more can you handle? How many hours are there in the day to create, manage, sell, and promote the book while also doing your day job?

You are right to believe that there is plenty of work to be done. This work is one of the reasons that a publisher takes such a large share of the revenue generated by a book. They are hiring the specialized people that it takes to do everything you are learning about in this book and more.

I think the most valuable web presences for your book are actually the cheapest and easiest to create. Your book can have a Facebook page and a blog absolutely free. These services provide easy-to-use online tools to build and maintain the content and the style of the site.

Facebook® Page

There are currently over 750 million Facebook users in the world. Most of these are individual people who are exchanging messages, photos, and games with their family, friends, and neighbors. But some of the pages are for companies, products, and books. You can use Facebook, MySpace, and other social networking services to create a presence for your book. It is a great way to pull together a social network of your readers and fans. The people who read your books are a social network. They have at least one thing in common—they are interested in your book and hopefully they can spread that interest to other people. But your fans have to be able to find each other and know where they can refer others who might be interested.

You can create a Facebook page for your book and begin friending the pages of other books and other people that you like. Begin by friending all of the people who are committed to supporting your work—your family, friends, and coworkers. That small core will help you get started in spreading the word.

Any time you are interviewed, do a book signing, or have a chance to pass out literature, make sure that you mention your book's Facebook page. These networks are like snowballs.

Each one begins with a small circle of friends, but it spreads rapidly from friend to friend until there are literally thousands of connections.

If you plan to write multiple books, then you might prefer to create a page for your publishing company or one that is focused on you as an author. Otherwise you may find yourself maintaining individual sites for two, three, or four different books which can be time consuming.

Check with each social network for their policies on hosting pages for books and other "non-human" entities.

Blog Pages

There are dozens of blogging services that offer free accounts and free storage for your postings. These allow you to create a unique visual design as well. It has become common for authors and other users to side-step all of the expenses and work associated with creating a unique web site by using free blogging services as an alternative. A well designed blog site is difficult to differentiate from a fully owned web domain.

With a blog you settle for a web address that is a little less unique. Rather than creating "my-press.com" or "my-book.com", you will have:
my-press.blogspot.com, or
my-book.wordpress.com.

Using tools like Blogger®, Word Press®, or Live Journal® you can create almost all of the web site features that come with a dedicated domain address, but at no cost. Some of the most popular blogging services are:

- Blogger—http://www.blogger.com/
- Word Press—http://www.wordpress.com/
- Live Journal—http://www.livejournal.com/

Amazon AuthorCentral

There is an entire chapter dedicated to services provided by Amazon.com. One of those is AuthorCentral which allows you to create a web page at the Amazon.com site that describes you as an author. It also pulls together all of the books you have written and provides a blogging service for you to attract and converse with your readers.

The Amazon AuthorCentral blogging service has the advantage that it is not another stand-alone web site lost among the millions of sites on the internet. It is integrated into Amazon's book catalog and linked to every one of your books. It puts you on "Book Main Street." You are much more likely to build a following through this service than through your own blogging site.

http://authorcentral.amazon.com/.

Unique Web Site

Some authors prefer to have an entire web site dedicated to their work. Luckily, creating a web site becomes easier every year. But it also becomes less necessary as social networks, blogs, and other variations become the preferred space for human interactions on the web.

If you feel that you must create a unique web site, then you can be comforted by the fact that the job is now within the means of most people. What used to require a very unique set of programming skills can be accomplished with a few point-and-click tools. You do not need to hire a web site designer or learn to write HTML code yourself to get a web site up and running.

There are a number of web site hosting services that will help you with every piece of the puzzle. Specifically you will need:

1. *Domain Name.* This is the address for your web site—such as www.ibm.com or www.modelbenders.com. These names are purchased from a registrar who insures that none of the names are being used in more than one place.

2. *Domain or Website Hosting.* Once you own a name, you need a place to host that name and all of the content that you want to appear on the web site. You can rent this by the month from thousands of different providers.

3. *Email Manager.* One of the big advantages of owning your own domain name is the ability to create an email address that is fitting for your publishing company—such as roger@modelbenders.com or me@my-press.com. This gives you a little more professional face in dealing with the publishing industry.

Competition has driven the price of these web services down until they are almost free. In fact, some companies do provide them completely free. If you are new to the idea of owning and creating your own web site, I would recommend that you check out some of the following offerings that are very affordable and easy to use.

- Dreamhost®—http://www.dreamhost.com/
- Go Daddy®—http://www.godaddy.com
- 1-and-1®—http://www.1and1.com/

Each of these providers has a wide range of services available. In some cases they have so many that it is mind boggling. GoDaddy® advertises so many options that visiting their web site is like walking through a carnival with the barkers calling for your attention in every direction. I would advise that, as with any carnival, you do not need most of the products that are being sold.

Money	Time
$0 Facebook page. $0 Blog Page. $10 per year for a Domain Name. $100 per year for Domain Hosting.	1 day to load your profile. 1 day to create the blog. 1 day to purchase. 3-4 weeks to get it up and running smoothly.

Chapter 14

Logo Therapy

Part III: Promoting

If you have decided to create "My Press" to sell your books, then you might want your own company logo. You will find dozens of useful places to use one. It can appear on the back cover of your book, your web site, blog, Facebook page, business cards, and email signature.

But how do you get a nice logo designed? You could use an Elance project to hire a designer. You might even include this task in the design project for the book itself. Or, you could try something more unique.

Logo Competition

What if you could get a lot of designers to compete against each other to give you a great logo? That is the idea behind LogoTournament.com®. This web site is similar to Elance in that it allows you to post a project and have multiple vendors bid on the work. But, at Logo Tournament, the bidders are creating logo designs in an attempt to win a competition. The prize is an amount of money that you put up to attract the talent.

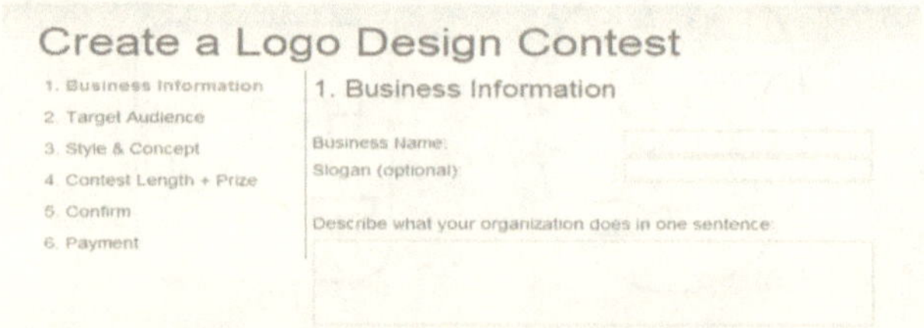

Figure 17-1. Logo Tournament Data Entry

The advantage of Logo Tournament is that you see dozens of different designs from scores of designers. During the competition you are able to comment on each submission and rank it based on your preferences. These rankings heat up the competition and generate even better submissions. I created a logo competition with a cash prize of $275 for a company logo. It attracted over 30 competitors who submitted 90 different logo concepts. This was a much more creative brainstorming process than I would have had on Elance. At Elance I would have selected a single designer from several bids and then relied on just one person to come up with a good design. But with Logo Tournament I saw the best ideas from 30 different creative people.

These competitions also attract designers from around the world. I received bids from Thailand, the Philippines, China, India, Canada, Great Britain, and the United States. The designs reflected the cultural styles of these countries.

Communicating Feel

Like most project web sites, Logo Tournament allows you to write a description of the company, project, or book for which the logo is being created (Figure 17-1). But the creators of Logo Tournament also recognized that artists need to know what kind of feeling or spirit that you imagine for your logo. They created a unique set of "Stylistic Sliders" to help you communicate this feel to the artists (Figure 17-2). This forces you to think through your own feelings and express them so that the artists can work in the right direction.

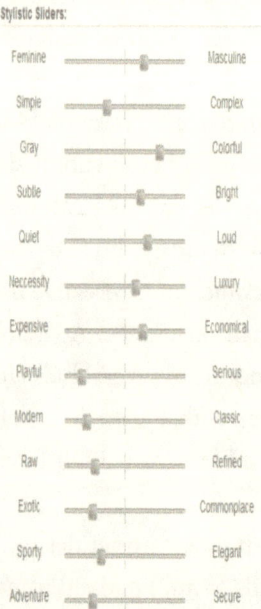

Figure 17-2. Logo Tournament Style Sliders

Should your logo have a feminine or masculine feel to it? Do you prefer something that is simple or more complex? Would you like many colors, or just shades of grey? Should the logo be quiet or loud? All of these communicate information that you would not think to put into a written description.

Feedback

Once the logo designs start to roll in, you need to be on top of the submissions. You must play an active role in posting comments to let the artists know what you think of their work. You can rank the designs that you like the best and decline those that are not appropriate. All of the artists see these preferences and shift in your direction like a cloud of gnats on a hot summer day. By the end you will have at least half a dozen really good concepts in the mixture.

Winner

When you select a winner, that artist will prepare the final graphic file formats for you. These can be used directly by book designers, web sites, and printers. I would recommend that you request both the raw file formats (e.g. EPS, AI), as well as a JPEG and PDF format. The latter formats are most useful on web sites, blogs, and business cards.

Withdrawn Entries

The competitors on Logo Tournament can be a bit temperamental. When they see their designs falling to the bottom of the rankings, they will often withdraw an entry. This will reduce the number of low scores that appear in their own profiles. It also allows them to reuse the same basic concept for another customer. Once an entry is withdrawn it will be erased from your project web page.

Logo Tournament is a great way to trigger a worldwide brainstorming session focused on your company logo.

Money	Time
$275 competition award.	21 days.

Chapter 15

Adding it Up

Once you have a published book, publishing company, and logo you are all set to begin marketing with printed materials. Your first step might be to print some business cards for your role as author and publisher. Today's self-service printers on the web can create cards that are more professional than the ones you receive from your daytime employer.

There are literally hundreds of printers to choose from online. They are all competing to provide unique, high quality products at discount prices. The competition among them is so fierce that you should have no problem finding good candidates simply by googling for "Business Card Printer" and other similar terms.

Moo.com®

Moo.com provides some unique products. There are two unusual sizes of business cards that are meant to grab people's attention. These are the half-sized and the over-sized, neither of which is the American standard size. A key feature of their cards is that you can include graphic images on the back side. Customers may choose to use their business logo, pictures of superheroes, or cartoons. Moo.com's web site has dozens of license-free images available for your use, or you can upload your own.

As a published author a natural image for the backs of the over-sized cards is the cover of your book. Your cards can then introduce you by name, your publishing company, and your book all at the same time. Moo.com's unique printing system allows you to put any number of pictures on the back of a series of cards. I chose to create a set in which the cover of eight of my books appeared in sequence on the backs of the cards. This allowed me to give a card to someone based on the book that I thought would be most interesting to them.

Moo.com's business cards are extremely high quality and they charge a premium price for them.

Vistaprint®

For more standard business cards, post cards, and flyers I have been happy with the products and prices of VistaPrint®. This company has a huge selection of printed items to choose from. You can turn to them for your general purpose printed materials at very low prices.

However, there are dozens of competing companies on the Internet that provide similar services. You should search for a printer that best meets your own needs.

FedEx® Kinkos®

Finally, there is the FedEx Kinkos office store chain. They can provide face-to-face advice on your print job and a more convenient place to work on errors if any should occur.

When I created a two-sided bookmark to promote my publishing company, I actually found Kinkos' prices to be lower than those from online printers. So do not assume that everything is cheaper online. Check around before you choose a printer.

Money	Time
$21.99 for a pack of 50 Moo.com business cards.	5 days for delivery.

Chapter 16

FaceSpace

Part III: Promoting

Do you use social networks like Facebook® and MySpace®? Have you created your own page on one of these sites that is dedicated to your book? If so, then you might be a good candidate for advertising on the social networks. If you use these sites then you have seen the type of advertising that appears along side of the content. Does your book fit into that style of advertising? If so, then the social network may have other users that would be customers for your book. If not, then it would probably be a waste of your time and money to advertise there.

As a small publisher you cannot afford to put your message in front of all 750 million users of Facebook. Luckily, the advertising engine for the site allows you to focus your ads on a specific demographic. This can be helpful if your book is targeted at "High School students in Michigan" or "22 year old professionals looking for apartments in New York City". But if your book is targeted at "Accountants working in mergers and acquisitions", then you will not find the tools very useful.

Most social networking sites, including Facebook and MySpace, allow you to create a commercial account for advertising. These sites also carry a standard set of rules on advertising that prohibit the offering of "Free, Free, Free Books", "You can get Rich in Your Sleep", and similarly misleading bait to get people to click on your advertisement.

Facebook®

You may have noticed that all of the ads that appear on your own Facebook pages look very similar. The site allows you to create an ad that is composed of a title, graphic, and short text message. Everyone gets the same format.

You are allowed 25 characters in the title and 135 characters in the text of the advertisement. The graphic must be 110 pixels x 80 pixels. Every ad that is submitted goes through a human review to insure that it does not violate the Facebook terms of service and is not believed to be misleading. The terms of service are very typical of what you would expect from a public web site. They must be honest and not contain misleading claims about your product. Facebook prohibits twenty different categories of content in its ads. These include profanity, obscenity, tobacco products, firearms, and chain letters. A detailed description of their guidelines can be found at:

http://www.facebook.com/ad_guidelines.php

MySpace®

Ads on MySpace have a different style from Facebook. They are predominantly graphic images. The MySpace ad tools allow you to put your own text on top of stock graphics available on their web site, or to upload your own custom graphic advertisement. There are more than a dozen different ad sizes and formats. MySpace ads can include video and audio and are allowed to expand and float over the page content.

A detailed description of MySpace ad requirements can be found at:

http://www.myspace.com/adspecs

My Experience

I have used both sites to advertise seminars for college students in specific cities. The tools allowed me to specify that the ads would appear only on the pages of users of a certain age who were attending college and living in my targeted city.

On Facebook and MySpace I specified the advertising budget that I was willing to spend for one month. My preference was to pay for clicks rather than for impressions. So I paid the site only when someone clicked on my ad, not when it merely appeared on their page. In both cases, I attracted enough clicks to completely spend my advertising budget for the month.

However, the advertising did not result in any registrations for the seminars. I was able to track the source of each person who came to my seminar registration page and none of them came from the major social networks. My experience is that I was able to attract attention on the social networks, but that attention did not translate into revenue. Based on advertising for four different seminars, I believe that most people on these sites are accustomed to getting everything for free. They are not visiting Facebook pages as shoppers. Some ads do grab their attention and cause them to click out of curiosity. But I believe they are looking for more free services. I do not think they are actively in "buying mode." It is quite difficult to shift their mind from "free fun" on social networks to purchasing products and services.

If you are a frequent user of a social network, ask whether you have ever made a purchase from these ads? I believe your own experience is a good indicator of what you can expect from the other 750 million users.

If you are not a frequent user of a social network, then I suggest that you are not in a position to create an effective advertisement for the site either.

Money	Time
$0 to learn.	1 day to learn.

Chapter 17

The Big Show

BookExpo America

There are a number of book conferences at which you can promote your book. The biggest and best attended of these is BookExpo America in New York City each May. This show attracts all of the famous writers, publishers, and a number of celebrities that like to hang out around books. You will find thousands of people just like you who are eager to make their mark in the book world. It is an extravaganza of energy around the written word.

This is where publishers and distributors come to look for promising books. You are looking for representatives who will consider your book for distribution or acquisition. When you have a finished book in hand you are a much more attractive partner for these companies than if you are just presenting them with a raw manuscript.

The registration fee for BEA is quite reasonable, $100 to $150 depending on the category that you choose. The biggest expense will be your travel costs to, from, in, and around New York City. But you can work with the BEA conference organizers who have arranged fair prices with a number of local hotels.

New Title Showcase

If you cannot physically attend BEA, you can still send your book. The New Title Showcase is a "book buyer's bookstore" that is hosted at the conference. It is open to any book published in the previous year. If a publisher, distributor, or buyer takes an interest in your book they may wish to discuss the possibility of purchasing it from you or creating a partnership.

If you have followed all of the steps in the previous chapters, then you have a good feeling for the work required to create a book and get it noticed. When a third party calls to discuss doing some of this in exchange for a controlling interest in the book you are in a much better position to understand what they will be doing for you and why they are charging for those services.

The price to place one copy of one book in the New Title Showcase is $265. But if you have multiple books in print, you can purchase an entire shelf of eight titles for $845. These prices seem rather high for a small 12" wide space on a shelf. But it is a lot less expensive than attending in the flesh or renting your own booth space at the show for $2,000 or more. The New Title Showcase is the poor man's entry into the world of book selling and book buying.

Regional Shows

There are a number of smaller regional shows at which you can exhibit and promote your work. If you are looking for events in your own geographic area, try searching for a local writers association. They usually sponsor these local events and will certainly be able to point you toward many more in the area.

Google "Florida Writers Association", but using the city or state where you live.

These shows are an invaluable source of ideas and contacts. If you are serious about selling your book you need to attend at least one. You will meet dozens or hundreds of independent authors and publishers who are in the same situation that you are. You can learn from their experiences and their mistakes.

Writers Associations

Though this book is specifically about getting your book published and noticed, you should know that there are thousands of independent authors all around you. You can find many of them in the local writers associations. These exist in every state and are concentrated around every major city. The number of people writing and publishing their own work is huge.

If you feel like you are alone in your quest to publish a book, it is because you have not tried hard enough to find the kindred souls that are just around the corner, down the block, and across town. When you find a local writers association you will uncover a pool of people who are eager to help and encourage you. These authors come together to create workshops, seminars, newsletters, and regular meetings. The association's web site is often a bookstore for the works of its members, allowing you to see what other writers have produced, and to promote your own work.

I have been encouraged by the Florida Writers Association. Specifically, one of the regular newsletter columns entitled "The First Million Words Don't Count". As unprepared as I often feel to launch a new book, I always remind myself that the only way to get good at writing it to write and the only way to learn to produce good books is to practice it. If some of my grammar and phrasing is bad, I don't stop writing, I just remind myself that the first million words do not count, and keep on going.

Money	Time
$45 for membership in a local writers association.	1 hour.
$265 for the BEA New Title Showcase.	1 day to create material for the Showcase.
$150 for registration at BEA.	
$2,000 for travel to New York City.	5 days to attend the whole event.

Chapter 18

Aaaaa Bbbbb Aaaaa

The American Booksellers Association (http://www.bookweb.org/) is the national trade association for independent booksellers. It offers education, products, advocacy, and relevant business information to independent bookstore owners. It targets small mom-and-pop bookstore owners. The association provides a unified voice for its members to larger vendors and to the government in Washington D.C. It also provides educational services that help small bookstore owners structure and operate their businesses.

You are an independent author, publisher, and online bookstore owner. If you plan to focus on the selling side of this role, you might benefit from membership in the ABA.

Membership also includes a free registration at BookExpo America, which is equal to about half of the ABA membership fee.

Educational Events

ABA has developed an educational curriculum that is focused on finances, store operations, and marketing. It presents a number of events that focus on specific needs of a bookstore or bookseller. The Winter Institute is a free two-day education program with more than twenty education sessions, social events, and networking opportunities for owners and staff of ABA member bookstores. The Spring Bookseller Forums are held in conjunction with regional booksellers associations. These forums provide opportunities for ABA members to receive updates on the Association's programs and initiatives, to voice their concerns, and to offer input on the future direction of ABA. BookExpo America is the largest English-language book industry event in the world. It contains over 2,000 publisher exhibits, more than 50 educational sessions, ABA's day-long education program of seminars and panel discussions, a specially-priced hotel exclusively for ABA member booksellers, and author autographing sessions. Also in conjunction with BEA, ABA holds its Town Hall and Annual meetings, the "Celebration of Bookselling" event, and a four-day school for people interested in opening a bookstore. ABA members receive discounted admission to BEA. ABA also provides members with a variety of distance learning opportunities, all accessible from BookWeb.org.

Industry Information

The *ABA Book Buyer's Handbook* is an online, searchable, and continuously updated resource for ordering and returns information. This electronic publication features publishers' trade terms, including discount schedules, returns policies, imprint and ISBN prefix listings, co-op policies and more, as well as timely special offers.

Bookselling This Week is the free web-based news outlet of ABA. It provides breaking news, coverage of key industry events and trends, updates on ABA and IndieBound, and in-depth feature articles about all aspects of bookselling. *BTW* headlines are also disseminated via a free weekly e-mail.

Advocacy

ABA devotes a large portion of its resources to advocating within the publishing industry and at all levels of government for the rights of independent booksellers and the protection of consumer privacy. Whether the issue is working towards a level playing field for all booksellers and against anticompetitive mergers and acquisitions, or for fair e-commerce taxation, literacy initiatives, Small Business Health Plan legislation, and the protection of First Amendment Rights, ABA vigorously represents the interests of independent booksellers.

These are the primary services and benefits of ABA. They are not specifically geared toward one-title authors, publishers, and online booksellers. But they do offer a window into the publishing and bookselling world that you might not otherwise be aware of.

Money	Time
$350 for full membership Or $200 for individual membership.	1 hour.

PART IV

Selling

Close the sale and deliver the product.

Chapter 19

Navigating the Amazon

Now that you are an author, the online bookstores want your attention. They have created special services to allow you to make your book entries more attractive on their sites. Amazon.com is one of the leaders in tools that will help you sell your book through their web site.

Amazon AuthorCentral

AuthorCentral allows you as an author to create a customized web site to collect all of your works and to write a biography to share with your readers. This service can be found at: http://authorcentral.amazon.com/.

Before you create your own profile on this site, take a few minutes to locate the profiles of some of your favorite authors. Search for one of their books on Amazon.com and scan down the page until you find the link to the author's profile—this is their AuthorCentral information. Notice the kind of information that they share about themselves and the voice that they use. Look at the style of photo that they have chosen to use. This is the kind of image that you want to create with your own AuthorCentral page.

Notice that the AuthorCentral page also contains a blog with which you can carry on a conversation with your readers. You may choose to load just a few key blog entries that will remain on the site for weeks. Or you can carry on a running discussion about your work. It is all up to you.

Amazon Associates

Amazon encourages the owners of web sites to direct shopping traffic to them for purchases. For example, when you visit the web site of a professional association you might find that it lists several good books on the subject of welding, computer programming, or investing. If you click on the links for those books, that web site might direct you to Amazon.com to make the purchase.

In exchange for this redirection to their site, Amazon.com pays the web site owner a small percentage of the sale that results if that person buys the book. This is called the Amazon Associates program. You can take advantage of this as well. It does not matter to Amazon that you happen to be the author of the book that is being sold. They are happy to give you a small commission if your web site sends them a paying customer. Remember that they purchase the book at a 55% discount, so they have a large margin of profit to share with associates who send them business.

If you choose not to do your own order fulfillment on your web site, you can get a little extra revenue from Amazon.com by using the Amazon Associates program. You could be sending them this traffic from your Facebook page, Blog, or web site.

Once you signup as an Amazon Associate you will find instructions on how to tag the links from your web site to the Amazon site so that you are credited with any sale that takes place. Begin at: https://affiliate-program.amazon.com/

Your Amazon Associates account can be the same account that you use to purchase books and that you used to join AuthorCentral. You might begin to notice that Amazon.com is offering a lot of services to make their site more attractive and useful to people like you. They are competing for market share with all of the other online bookstores, and they are using their expertise in information technology to give them an edge.

Amazon Advertising Widgets

Amazon Associates are given access to some very cool tools for creating advertisements to appear on their Facebook, Blog, or web site. These tools create an advertisement that is much more attractive than the one you were going to make yourself. Using a set of menus you create a fancy display advertisement on the Amazon Associates web site and they generate the HTML code for the ad. All you have to do is copy the code and paste it onto your own web page. This will cause the fancy Amazon advertisement to appear on your site.

Let Amazon help you sell your books with these tools. As an independent author and publisher you need all of the help that you can get, and it is rare to find a big partner like Amazon who will offer their help for free.

Money	Time
$0.	1 day.

Chapter 20

Money Money Money

Who is selling your book?

You have already learned how to get your book listed at online bookstores like Amazon.com. Each time someone places an order for the book on those sites, it is routed to Lightning Source. They fill the order on behalf of the online bookstore and credit your account for the sale. If your book retails for $7.95 and you have assigned it a wholesale discount of 55%, then each time one copy is sold 45% of the money is yours and 55% of the retail price was discounted to leave room for the bookstore to make a profit. So for each copy the online bookstore pays Lightning Source:

$$\$7.95 * 45\% = \$3.58$$

Remember that each copy of the book costs something to be printed by LSI. If your book is 110 pages long as we have assumed earlier, then the production cost of that book was 90 cents for the cover and 1.3 cents for each page, or:

$$\$0.90 + \$0.013 * 110 = \$2.33$$

Assume that the book was sold at its full retail price. In that case the money would be divided as shown in Table 14-1.

Table 14-1. Distribution of Book Revenue at Full Retail Price

Recipient	Revenue
Lightning Source	$2.33
You as the Publisher/Author	$1.25
Online Bookstore	$4.37
State Sales Tax at 6%	$0.48
Total Sales Price	**$8.43**

You will notice that the largest portion of the price of the book goes to the bookstore, in this case an online bookstore like Amazon. Because publishers give these bookstores such a large discount on the retail price, they actually have the leeway to offer the book at a discount to the retail price. When you see a book at an online bookstore selling at a discount to its retail price, they are generally buying the book at the standard 55% discount, but have chosen to reduce the amount that they make on each sale in order to attract more customers.

When you created a web site for your book or publishing company you not only created a promotional site, you also created an alternate site through which you could sell the book yourself. Your web site is essentially a very small online bookstore that just carries one book.

Many small authors are eager to sell through their own site because it allows them to earn the 55% of retail price that was previously in the pockets of Amazon.com and Barnes & Noble

Online. So let's look at the distribution of the revenue if you sell the book yourself at full retail price.

Table 14-2. Distribution of Book Revenue through your Web Site

Recipient	Revenue
Lightning Source	$2.33
You as the Publisher/Author	$1.25
Your Own Online Bookstore	$4.37
State Taxes at 6%	$0.48
Total Sales Price	**$8.43**

As the publisher you now earn the full retail price of the book minus the cost that you pay for Lightning Source to produce it. Potentially you are now making $1.25 + $4.37, or $5.62 on the sale of each copy. This is too attractive for some self-publishers to pass up. The additional $4.37 might be enough to pay for all of the costs that you incur to create and maintain the web site for the book.

If you are making $5.62 on the sale of each book at $7.95, that leaves a lot of room for you to discount the price of the book on your web site. At the extreme you could even choose to sell the book at a $4.37 discount, giving the customer a huge discount and trimming your share back to the original $1.25 that you received when Amazon.com sold the book.

Before you jump into filling your own orders, you need to understand a few important details.

PayPal®

If you are going to sell products, then you need some method to accept payment via credit card. Most small businesses use PayPal® for this. They are the broker of funds between two parties on thousands of web sites, most prominently eBay®. You can use their services just as millions of others have before you.

To do this you need to create an account at PayPal.com. If you already have a personal account for making purchases online, you can upgrade it to allow you to receive payment as well. You are essentially joining the ranks of all of the sellers that you see on eBay.

In exchange for the services that PayPal provides you will pay them a small transaction fee and a small percentage of the price of your product. The size of the fees depends on the number of transactions that you have through PayPal and the kind of plan that you choose to arrange with them.

For a book selling at $7.95, PayPal would charge you a transaction fee of 30 cents, and 2.9% of the cover price of the book. This would be just 53 cents. But check PayPal's current rates and the different agreements available to get the latest fees.

Taxes

Paying local sales taxes for online transactions has been an issue ever since online retail began nearly two decades ago. In fact, it was an issue for mail order catalogs and telephone vendors for a century before online retail came along. The general rule is that you must collect sales tax when you sell a book to someone who is in the same state that your publishing company is in. This rule also applies to all of the vendors who post their goods on eBay.

The state governments have a difficult time enforcing this rule; so many small vendors choose to ignore it. This is not a good idea and I do not recommend it for your new "My Press" web site. Eventually, the tax man will catch up with you and there will be an unpleasant financial adjustment to contend with. If you are selling books through your web site, you should collect the appropriate sales taxes and then pass those on to the state government.

PayPal offers several simple forms that allow you to collect taxes only from specific buyers. Setting up the collection for people in a specific state is not difficult.

However, passing that money on to the state government can be difficult. Before you collect taxes, you are usually required to register your business with the state and file a request to collect taxes. Once this is approved, the state will expect you to file forms and make payments to them every quarter.

I found these regulations to be too onerous. It appeared to me that I would be spending too much time on paperwork to justify the additional revenue. To avoid this I chose to route buyers from my web site to Amazon.com. That means Amazon is handling all of the tax issues. I am not able to capture the additional $4.37 per book, but I escape the entanglements of dealing directly with the tax man.

You could choose to sell books through your web site, but only to people residing outside of your home state. Your web site might read *"For Purchases in the State of Florida Click Here to purchase at Amazon.com."* This would allow you to split the business in into two pieces and avoid the sales tax issue. I chose not to do this because there are 50 different states and each has different tax laws. I thought that Amazon would be better at complying with all of these than I would. So I route all sales to Amazon.com for the actual purchase. However, I plan to revisit this decision when I have the time to work through the details of state sales tax collection, reporting, and payment.

eBay's Half.com

Rather than selling your books through your own web site, you could choose to list them at self-serve web sites like eBay and Half.com® (a subsidiary of eBay). These allow you to post your item for sale, set your price, accept orders, and fulfill them yourself.

Posting the book at Half.com would allow many more people to find it when searching for used and discounted books. The transaction would be settled through PayPal just as I described above. But you are going to have to deal with the sales tax issue again.

Lightning Source Fulfillment

When you place an order for your own case of books on the LSI web site you will notice that the return address is that of your own publishing company. The web site it set up to allow you to place an order for shipment to anyone that you would like to receive it. You can do this for a case of books, a fractional case, or a single copy. In practice it is not economical for you to order a single copy from LSI and have it shipped directly to the person who placed the original order on your web site. It is generally more economical for you to purchase a case for delivery to your home, and then to use that stock to fill orders from your web site.

However, it may still be economical to use LSI to ship directly from the printer to a customer who orders for an entire case. This often happens when a bookstore, educational institution, or professional association buys a number of copies for their customers, students, or members.

When a customer is buying in large quantities, you can work with them to give a substantial discount to the single-copy price. You understand the costs described above and can do your own estimates on the size of the discount that you can afford to give them.

Money	Time
$0.	Many days.

Chapter 21

Wrap it Up

Part IV: Selling

By this time you have found yourself in the role of author, publisher, promoter, and bookstore for your own books. This job has gotten a lot bigger than you expected when you started. At first, you just wanted to print up a case full of books to give to your relatives, post an entry on Amazon.com, and wait for millions of copies to be sold. But reaching that last goal is more work than writing the book itself.

Part of your job as the promoter of your work is to send sample copies to people who can get the word out. For a non-fiction book you might send copies to all of the professional associations that cover the topic area of the book, including trade magazines and college professors.

If you choose to sell copies of your book directly from your web site, Half.com, and Amazon's used book listings (the books do not actually have to be used), then you are going to have to equip yourself with the materials to ship an order out the door. You need padded envelopes, sticky labels, and a postal scale. All of these are readily available at your local office supply store. But they are also available at half those prices on eBay. I recommend that you find your materials online, rather than paying the premiums charged by the office supply stores.

Bubble Mailers

One of the standard book mailing envelopes is the 8.5" x 12" bubble mailer. A box of 100 of these envelopes is available on eBay for about $30. That is just 30 cents each. The same box at the office supply store will cost about $135, or $1.35 each. Or you can buy them one at a time for about $1.80.

Remember that the cost of the envelope is added directly to the price that you have to charge your customers for shipping and handling. They are certainly much happier paying 30 cents for the bubble mailer that they are going to throw away, rather than $1.35.

Shipping Labels

You will be printing shipping labels from your own computer. The standard size shipping labels are 5.5" x 8.5" so two of them fit onto a single sheet of paper. At eBay you can purchase 100 sheets, or 200 labels, for about $5.50. The same product in a name brand at the office supply store cost about $52. So you can choose to put 3 cents into each label, or 26 cents. The online price is almost one tenth of the retail price. Again, this is a product that is going to be thrown away after use.

Postal Scale

An electronic postal scale on eBay sells for around $20. A similar scale at the office supply store is between $55 and $65. The two products are almost identical.

Purchasing Postage

You will not find any online vendors of books, antiques, clothes, or electronics standing in the service line at the local post office. Those lines are for amateurs. Once you have your own envelopes, labels, and a scale you are your own post office.

When a customer makes a purchase from your web site or Half.com they are directed to pay you via PayPal. Then you can use PayPal's built in postage system to print the mailing label with the proper postage on your home computer. The 5.5" x 8.5" labels described above are the standard size used by both the PayPal and the US Postal Service's web postage systems.

If you are sending complimentary copies of your book to trade magazines or professional associations, you cannot use the PayPal site to print the label because the order did not come through the PayPal billing system. But the U.S. Post Office has the identical service available on their web site, under "Print Shipping Labels." You can create an account on their web site and use it to buy postage and print your shipping labels at home, just as you do with PayPal's system.

These two services allow you to completely bypass the long lines at the Post Office, which is good for you and good for all of those people that have to stand in the line. They will not be looking at the back of your head and wondering how long your order is going to hold them up.

Media Rate Postage

The US Postal Service® provides a special rate for shipping media, which includes books, film, manuscripts, sound recordings, video tapes, and computer readable media (such as CDs, DVDs, and diskettes). These prices are much lower than the standard rates.

A small book of around 110 pages will weigh less than a pound. So postage for this book will be $2.38 or less using the media rate. Regular postage for a one pound package is $4.90. So the media rate is about half of the regular rate.

The PayPal shipping system includes the media mail rate as an option on their web site. So the orders that are purchased through PayPal can take advantage of this bargain. Curiously, the media mail rates are not offered through the U.S. Postal System (USPS) web site. Even though they invented the program, it is not included in their online postage system. To get this rate when purchasing postage directly from the USPS you have to go into one of their branches and stand in the line. There is no explaining how the government works.

Money	Time
$30 for Bubble Mailers. $5 for Shipping Labels. $20 for an Electronic Postal Scale.	1 hour.

PART V

Legalizing

Exercise your legal muscles to protect your book.

Chapter 22

To the Library

When you have poured your heart and soul into a book, the last thing you want is to see someone steal the contents outright and try to sell it. What can you do to prevent this?

Did you know that when you write anything on your own time, the copyright for it automatically belongs to you? But if you are writing for an employer who is paying by the hour, by the word, or by the year for your services, then the result is a "work for hire" which means that the rights belong to your employer. But your own work is your property in the same way that a piece of homemade furniture or clothing would be. When you turn raw materials into a new product, it is yours. This includes turning the raw English language into a written book.

Library of Congress Registration

If copyright is automatically granted to your work as soon as you write it, then why should you go to the trouble to register your copyright with the American Library of Congress, or a similar body in other countries?

Registration is a means of officially and publicly identifying the work as yours and identifying the date on which it was created. If there is a dispute over the first author of a piece of text, the registration process provides the legal system with proof of ownership and the date of that ownership. Registered copyrights have a much stronger standing in legal actions that could emerge.

You can register your work through the Copyright.gov web site. All of the steps to do this are web-based, so you do not have to work with paper forms at all. Select the "eCO" icon on the web site to enter the "Electronic Copyright Office."

Once you have completed the online registration process, you will print a data sheet to attach to one copy of your book, which you will mail to the copyright office. It usually takes them several months to process your application and return a certificate of copyright registration.

The entire process for a printed book costs just $35.

Fair Use

Copyright means that other people or companies cannot copy your work without asking your permission and paying for the privilege if that is what you want. You probably remember your teachers in school emphasizing that you should not copy the work of other people. Strictly, that would be a violation of the copyright laws for which you could be sued. However, in practice, no author or publisher is interested in hiring lawyers to chase down children writing research papers. Also, the copyright laws allow for some "fair use" of material taken from your book.

Fair Use is a doctrine in the United States copyright law that allows limited use of copyrighted material without requiring permission from the copyright holder. Typical uses of this material include commentary, criticism, news reporting, research, teaching, or scholarship. Fair Use provides for the legal, non-licensed citation or incorporation of copyrighted material in another author's work under a four-factor balancing test.

> ### Four Factor Balancing Test in the US Copyright Act of 1976
>
> *"Notwithstanding the provisions of sections 17 U.S.C. § 106 and 17 U.S.C. § 106A, the fair use of a copyrighted work, including such use by reproduction in copies or phonorecords or by any other means specified by that section, for purposes such as criticism, comment, news reporting, teaching (including multiple copies for classroom use), scholarship, or research, is not an infringement of copyright. In determining whether the use made of a work in any particular case is a fair use the factors to be considered shall include:*
>
> 1. *the purpose and character of the use, including whether such use is of a commercial nature or is for nonprofit educational purposes;*
> 2. *the nature of the copyrighted work;*
> 3. *the amount and substantiality of the portion used in relation to the copyrighted work as a whole; and*
> 4. *the effect of the use upon the potential market for or value of the copyrighted work.*
>
> *The fact that a work is unpublished shall not itself bar a finding of fair use if such finding is made upon consideration of all the above factors."*

This description is not entirely clear without reading additional material in the Copyright Act. The four points try to emphasize that the purpose of your new work must be to make a contribution to society that is additive to what already exists. If you are attempting to copy existing work in order to supersede it, using the copied material to redirect people to your derivative work, then your use of the material is probably a violation of copyright.

Frequently Asked Questions

There are several basic questions that every new author asks about copyright registration. These answers come from the web site of the United States Copyright Office.

What is copyright?

Copyright is a form of protection grounded in the U.S. Constitution and granted by law for original works of authorship fixed in a tangible medium of expression. Copyright covers both published and unpublished works.

What does copyright protect?

Copyright, a form of intellectual property law, protects original works of authorship including literary, dramatic, musical, and artistic works, such as poetry, novels, movies, songs, computer software, and architecture. Copyright does not protect facts, ideas, systems, or methods of operation, although it may protect the way these things are expressed.

How is a copyright different from a patent or a trademark?

Copyright protects original works of authorship, while a patent protects inventions or discoveries. Ideas and discoveries are not protected by the copyright law, although the way in which they are expressed may be. A trademark protects words, phrases, symbols, or designs identifying the source of the goods or services of one party and distinguishing them from those of others.

When is my work protected?

Your work is under copyright protection the moment it is created and fixed in a tangible form that it is perceptible either directly or with the aid of a machine or device.

Do I have to register with your office to be protected?

No. In general, registration is voluntary. Copyright exists from the moment the work is created. You will have to register, however, if you wish to bring a lawsuit for infringement of a U.S. work.

Why should I register my work if copyright protection is automatic?

Registration is recommended for a number of reasons. Many choose to register their works because they wish to have the facts of their copyright on the public record and have a certificate of registration. Registered works may be eligible for statutory damages and attorney's fees in successful litigation. Finally, if registration occurs within 5 years of publication, it is considered prima facie evidence in a court of law.

Is my copyright good in other countries?
The United States has copyright relations with most countries throughout the world, and as a result of these agreements, we honor each other's citizens' copyrights. However, the United States does not have such copyright relationships with every country.

Money	Time
$35 to register one book.	1 hour to complete form. 2 months waiting for certificate.

Chapter 23

Leaving Your Mark

In the United States there are three kinds of protected intellectual property—the copyright, trademark, and patent. The words of a book or song are covered by a copyright. Your company logo or slogan is covered by a trademark. A new mousetrap invention is covered by a patent. Each of these is handled by a different office with a different process and a different fee.

Trademark Protection

If you have created a logo or slogan for your publishing company you might consider registering these for trademark protection. When you want to protect a trademark you can attach the "TM" symbol to it to indicate that it is your trademark. This is something that you have complete discretion to do yourself without registration. However, if there is a legal dispute between two parties who believe that they have the first right to use a symbol, name, or phrase, then the legal system will look for a means to determine which party was the first to use the trademarked item in commerce.

> **Trademark Definition from US Trademark Office web site**
>
> *"Trademark protects words, names, symbols, sounds, or colors that distinguish goods and services from those manufactured or sold by others and to indicate the source of the goods. Trademarks, unlike patents, can be renewed forever as long as they are being used in commerce."*

The primary means of establishing your right to a trademark is to register it with the US Trademark Office. This creates an official record of your use of the mark. It also triggers a search of the trademark registration database to see if the mark has already been registered. If it has not, then your registration will probably be accepted. Often the trademark examiner will work with you to adapt your trademark claim to something that is genuinely and reasonably unique and defendable. When this process is done, you can apply the ® symbol to your trademark. This indicates that it is your trademark and that the mark has been successfully registered with the Trademark Office.

If you examine the packaging of most commercial products you will find the ® and ™ marks on several items on the package, including the:
- Company Logo
- Product Logo
- Company Slogan
- Product Slogan
- Company or Product Mascot

The price to register a trademark is currently $325, much higher than registering a copyright. This registration will protect your work for as long as you choose to renew the registration and claim to use it for commercial purposes. You are expected to renew your registration between the 5th and 6th year of the previous registration to maintain the uninterrupted rights to the mark.

> **A trademark is designated by one of the following symbols:**
>
> 1. ™ *for an unregistered trade mark used to promote or brand goods*
> 2. ℠ *for an unregistered service mark used to promote or brand services*
> 3. ® *for a registered trademark covering either goods or services*

Registration Process

The law considers a trademark to be a form of property. Proprietary rights in relation to a trademark may be established through actual use in the marketplace, or through registration of the mark with the trademarks office (or "trademarks registry") of a particular jurisdiction. Certain jurisdictions generally do not recognize trademarks rights arising through use. In the United States the only way to qualify for a federally registered trademark is to first use the trademark in commerce. If trademark owners do not hold registrations for their marks in such jurisdictions, the extent to which they will be able to enforce their rights through trademark infringement proceedings will be limited. In the case of a dispute, this disparity of rights is often referred to as "first to file" as opposed to "first to use."

Countries such as Germany offer a limited amount of common law rights for unregistered marks where to gain protection, the goods or services must occupy a highly significant position in the marketplace—which could be 40% or more market share for sales in the particular class of goods or services.

In the United States the registration process entails several steps prior to a trademark receiving its Certificate of Registration. These are described on the office's web site.

First, the individual or entity applying for the registration files an application to register the respective trademark. The application is then placed in line in the order it was received to be examined by an examining attorney for the U.S. Patent and Trademark Office.

Second, following a period of anywhere from three to six months the application is reviewed by an examining attorney to make sure that it complies with all requirements in order to be entitled to registration. This review includes procedural matters such as making sure the applicant's goods or services are identified properly. It also includes more substantive matters such as making sure the applicant's mark is not merely descriptive or likely to cause confusion with a pre-existing applied-for or registered mark. If the application runs afoul of any requirement, the examining attorney will issue an office action requiring the applicant to address certain issues or refusals prior to registration of the mark.

Third, after the examination of the mark has concluded with no issues to be addressed or an applicant has responded adequately to an examining attorney's concerns, the application will be published for opposition. During this 30-day period third-parties who may be affected by the registration of the trademark may step forward to file an Opposition Proceeding to stop the registration of the mark. If an Opposition Proceeding is filed, it institutes a case before the Trademark Trial and Appeal Board to determine both the validity of the grounds for the opposition as well as the ability of the applicant to register the mark at issue.

Fourth, provided that no third-party opposes the registration of the mark during the opposition period or the opposition is ultimately decided in the applicant's favor the mark will be registered in due course.

Outside of the United States the registration process is substantially similar to that found in the U.S. save for one notable exception in many countries: registration occurs prior to the opposition proceeding. In short, once an application is reviewed by an examiner and found to be entitled to registration a registration certificate is issued subject to the mark being open to opposition for a period of typically six months from the date of registration.

Usage Rights
A registered trademark confers a bundle of exclusive rights upon the registered owner, including the right to exclusive use of the mark in relation to the products or services for which

it is registered. The law in most jurisdictions also allows the owner of a registered trademark to prevent unauthorized use of the mark in relation to products or services which are identical or "colourfully" similar to the "registered" products or services, and in certain cases, prevent use in relation to entirely dissimilar products or services. The test is always whether a consumer of the goods or services will be confused as to the identity of the source or origin. An example may be a very large multinational brand such as "Sony" where a non-electronic product such as a pair of sunglasses might be assumed to have come from Sony Corporation of Japan despite not being a class of goods that Sony has rights in.

Once trademark rights are established in a particular jurisdiction, these rights are generally only enforceable in that jurisdiction, a quality which is sometimes known as territoriality. However, there is a range of international trademark laws and systems which facilitate the protection of trademarks in more than one jurisdiction.

Money	Time
$325 to register one trademark.	2 hours to complete form. 2 months waiting for certificate.

Chapter 24

Home Away From Home

Part V: Legalizing

Stephen King's home address is not printed on the copyright page of his books. Neither should yours be.

You have noticed that printing a book requires sharing your address with a very large audience. You need to put a mailing address on the copyright page of your book, in the contact information on your web site, in the copyright and trademark registration filings, as the address for your printing company, and a number of other places.

Do you want all of this attention focused on your home address? Do you want the place where you live, raise your childen, and walk your dogs to be the official location at which the world comes looking for the famous author?

Most of us have lives uninterrupted by inconveniences and dangers. However, I would recommend that the address that you use for your publishing company be different from your home address. This creates a very clean separation between your personal life and your public life. This distance can provide a little additional comfort and privacy.

Renting a post office or mail drop box is the least expensive and most convenient way to separate your personal and professional addresses. A small postal box at the USPS rents for between $50 and $75 a year. This is a very small price to pay for a business address that separates your business interests from your personal life.

Money	Time
$50 to $75.	1 hour.

Chapter 25

Ink Inc

Part V: Legalizing

You have created a unique name and logo for your publishing business, purchased a post office box, and printed business cards. Does this mean that you have created a separate company?

No, not yet.

At this point you are "doing business as". If I had named my publishing business "Rapid Publishers" and created a logo to appear on my business cards, it may look to the world like I am a corporation. But in the legal sense, Rapid Publishers is just a different name for Roger Smith the author and entrepreneur. This situation is usually described as "Roger Smith, doing business as Rapid Publishers."

The shorthand for "doing business as" is generally "d/b/a". There are many small businesses and one-man operations that function in this form for decades. It is perfectly legal and acceptable. You can create business cards, advertisements, and even open a bank account using the Rapid Publishers name.

However, a "d/b/a" is really just a trade name for you personally. It does not entitle you to a number of tax advantages that are available to corporations. It provides no protection from liability suits or other legal actions. It is difficult to separate the company's money from your own money.

My Press LLC

If you plan to operate "My Press" for a long period of time and are serious about making money with it, then you should consider creating a legal corporate entity to handle your money, file your taxes, and protect your personal wealth from the operations and liabilities of the business.

There are entire books on all of the different forms of corporations that are available to you. My advice is to begin as a Limited Liability Company (LLC). This form of business was practically custom made for small businesses like the one you are operating. The registration and operating fees are very low. The overhead paperwork is light. It opens the door to tax benefits afforded to a business. And finally, the money that the LLC makes is taxed only once, rather than twice as many large corporate profits are.

An LLC is a flexible form of business enterprise that blends elements of the partnership and corporate structures. Although a business entity, it is actually a type of unincorporated association and is not strictly a corporation. The primary characteristic that an LLC shares with a corporation is limited liability, and the primary characteristic it shares with a partnership is the availability of pass-through income taxation. It is often more flexible than a corporation and is well-suited for companies with a single owner.

To really understand the benefits of an LLC you need to read an entire book on the different business types that are available to you. You can also get a quick start by reading the Wikipedia entries on these topics, then searching the web for the many details that are already published there.

Advantages

LLCs in some states can be set up with just one natural person involved.

An LLC can elect to be taxed as a sole proprietor, partnership, S corporation, or C corporation, as long as they would otherwise qualify for such tax treatment.

Limited liability owners are protected from some or all liability for acts and debts of the LLC depending on state shield laws.

There is much less administrative paperwork and record keeping than a corporation.

Pass-through taxation allows the revenue of the corporation to be taxed only once when it is distributed to the owners, avoiding the initial taxation that C corporations pay when they earn the money.

Profits are taxed at the level of the owner who receives them, not at the level of earnings of the entire LLC. This can be significant when the LLC's revenue is split between multiple owners of an LLC.

LLCs in most states are treated as entities separate from their members. However, in some jurisdictions case law has developed deciding that LLCs are not considered to have separate legal standing from their members.

Membership interests of LLCs can be assigned, and the economic benefits of those interests can be separated and assigned, providing the assignee with the economic benefits of distributions of profits and losses like a partnership, but without transferring the title to the owner's interest.

Unless the LLC has chosen to be taxed as a corporation, income of the LLC generally retains its character, for instance as capital gains or as foreign sourced income, in the hands of the owners.

Registration

You may not need a lawyer, accountant, or consulting firm to help you create an LLC. In most states you can begin by visiting the web site of your state office of Revenue or Corporations—each state is slightly different. This site will provide you with the details that you need to file the paperwork to become an LLC.

Look for a link to "Articles of Organization" or a similar term.

In Florida, the forms are just a couple of pages of basic questions and statements about what the company intends to do and who the officers are. The filing fee is just $125. Then each year I have to renew the registration for $80. I also pay a county business tax of $25 per year.

Reporting

LLCs are required to produce an annual financial report for the business and distribute it to the partners. This identifies how much money the company made, what its expenses were, and how much will be distributed to the partners. This is the same information that you have to collect and report on your tax returns. So it is a good idea to create this report at the same time that you do your taxes.

Employer Identification Number

Every entity that earns money or owes taxes in the United States needs to have a Tax Identification Number (TIN). For you as an individual this is your Social Security Number. For a company which is established as a unique entity (not a d/b/a), this is the Employer Identification Number (EIN). The EIN uniquely identifies the entity to the government and is persistent as long as that entity exists. The number pulls together all of the money you make from various sources into a single account that can be tracked and taxed.

The EIN for your LLC must be obtained from the Internal Revenue Service. You will find details on applying for this number at the IRS.gov web site. Search for "EIN". The application can be filled out online. The IRS will verify the information and provide an EIN to you immediately. If there is some reason that you must submit your application for an EIN by mail, then it will take about four weeks for the IRS to process the paperwork and provide the number. If you can file those same paper forms by FAX, then you can shorten this time to just four days.

In all cases, you should read the legal status of an LLC for the state where you will register. You should also understand the IRS terms governing businesses like the LLC. All of this information is available on the web sites of these organizations.

Money	Time
$125 to register LLC. $80 for annual LLC renewal. $25 for annual county business tax. $0 for IRS EIN.	1 day to register. 1 hour to renew.

Chapter 26

End of the Beginning

Part V: Legalizing

This book has taken you through a formula for turning a draft manuscript into a printed case of books in just two months. I stuck to the essential steps so you could follow the process as easily as possible. I have used it many times myself. In the 21st century there are no barriers to stop you from creating your own book—except the barrier of ignorance. Now that you know how, all you need is about $1,000 to carry the process to completion.

Printing, promoting, and selling your own book is one of the most rewarding projects you can undertake. It is a huge milestone of empowerment in your life. Your ability to tackle such a significant project and carry it to completion is evidence that you are capable of even greater things. Use this to boost yourself to a new level of success in your life. Let this project convince you that you are capable of much more than you ever expected.

Many people are so excited upon finishing their first book that they immediately dive into a second. Whether you put your efforts into promoting a single masterpiece or multiple works, you are not the same person who began this project. You are now a much bigger and more capable person.

I have given you the process and the information that you need to produce a book in two months for about $1,000. Now it is time for you to do it yourself, to show the world what you are capable of, and to use this as a stepping stone to even greater accomplishments in the future.

Good luck and happy publishing.

www.ingramcontent.com/pod-product-compliance
Lightning Source LLC
LaVergne TN
LVHW091546060526
838200LV00036B/724